THE MONSTER KINGDOM OF
Kaiju Kittens

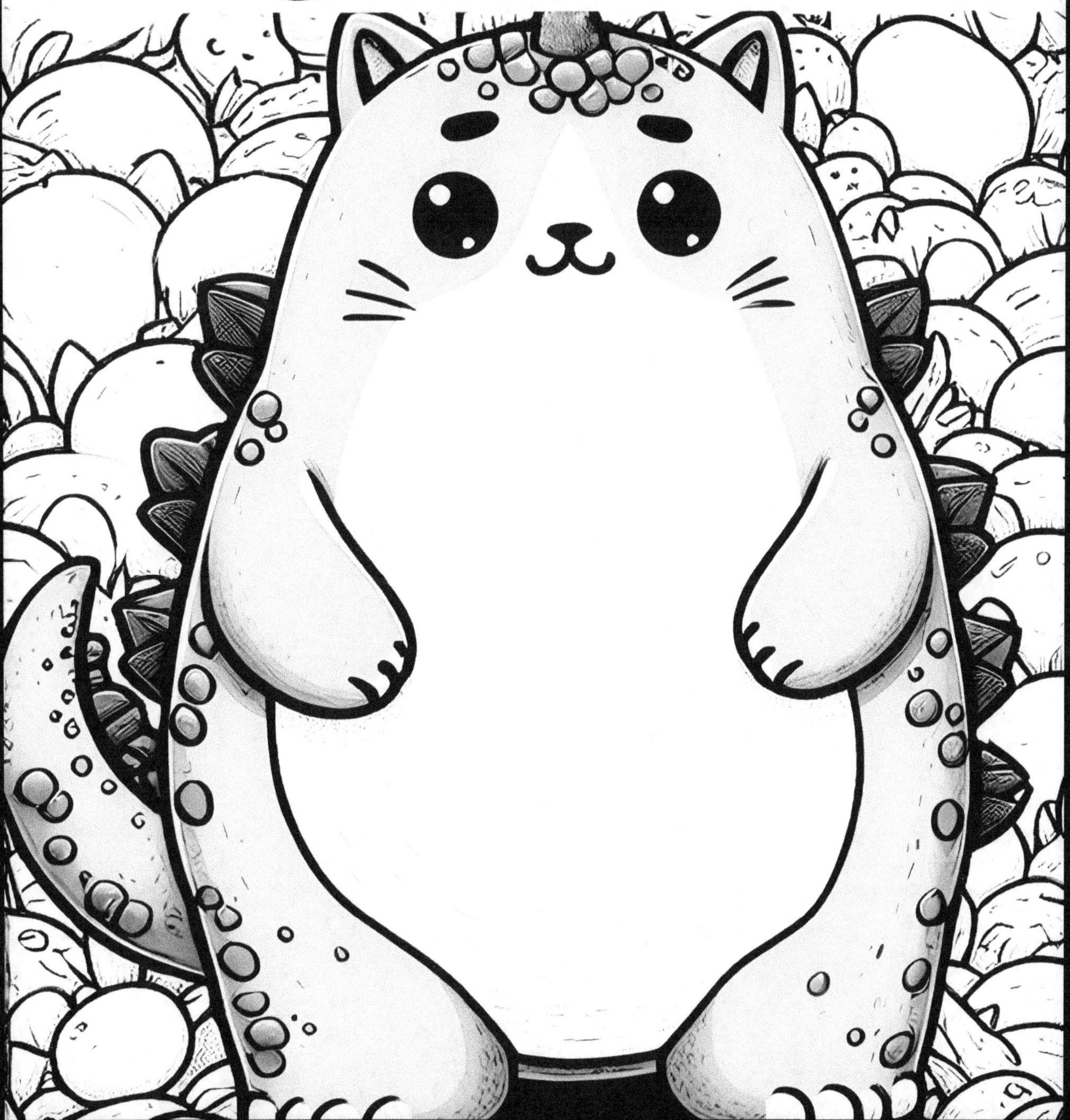

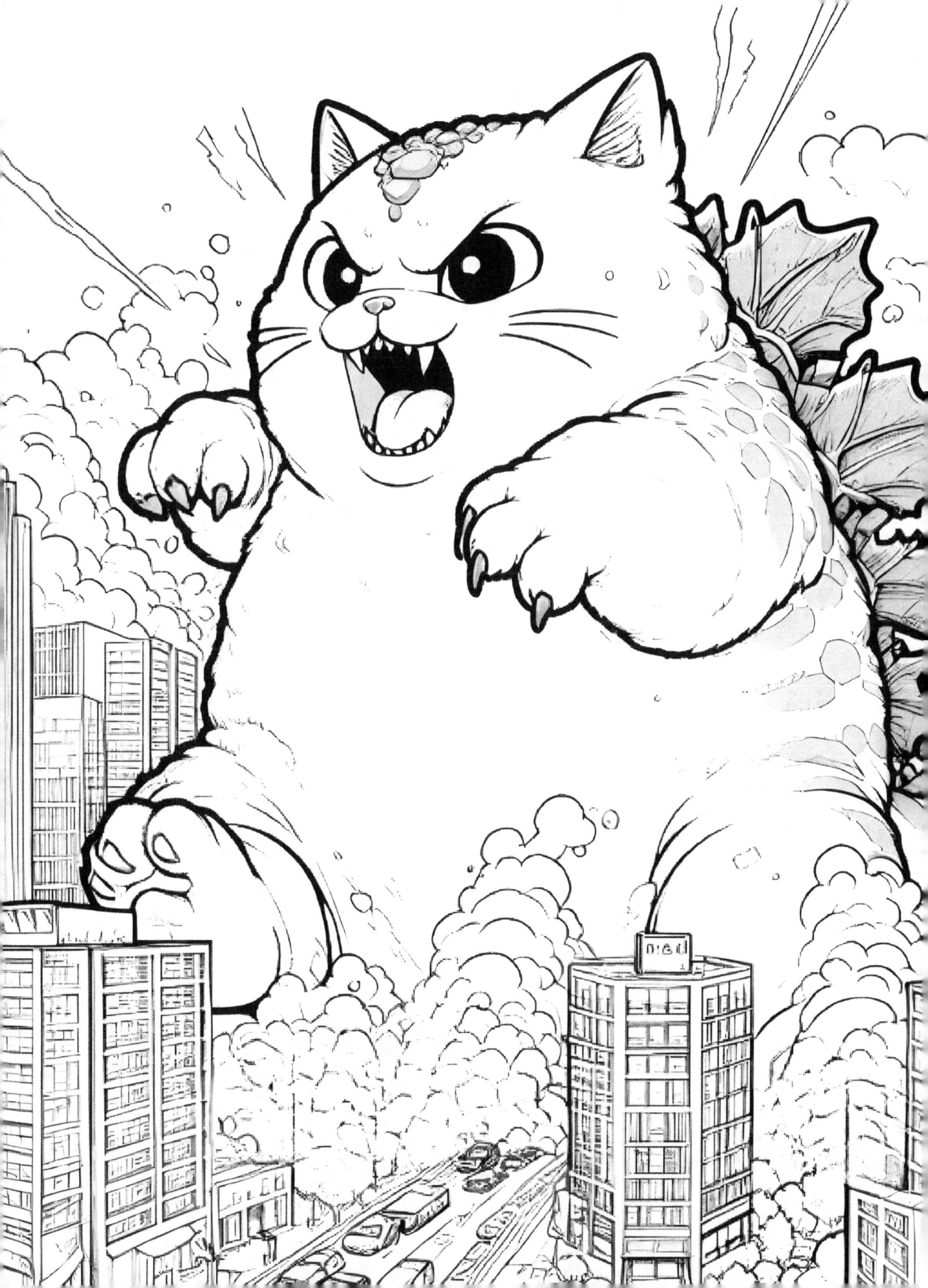

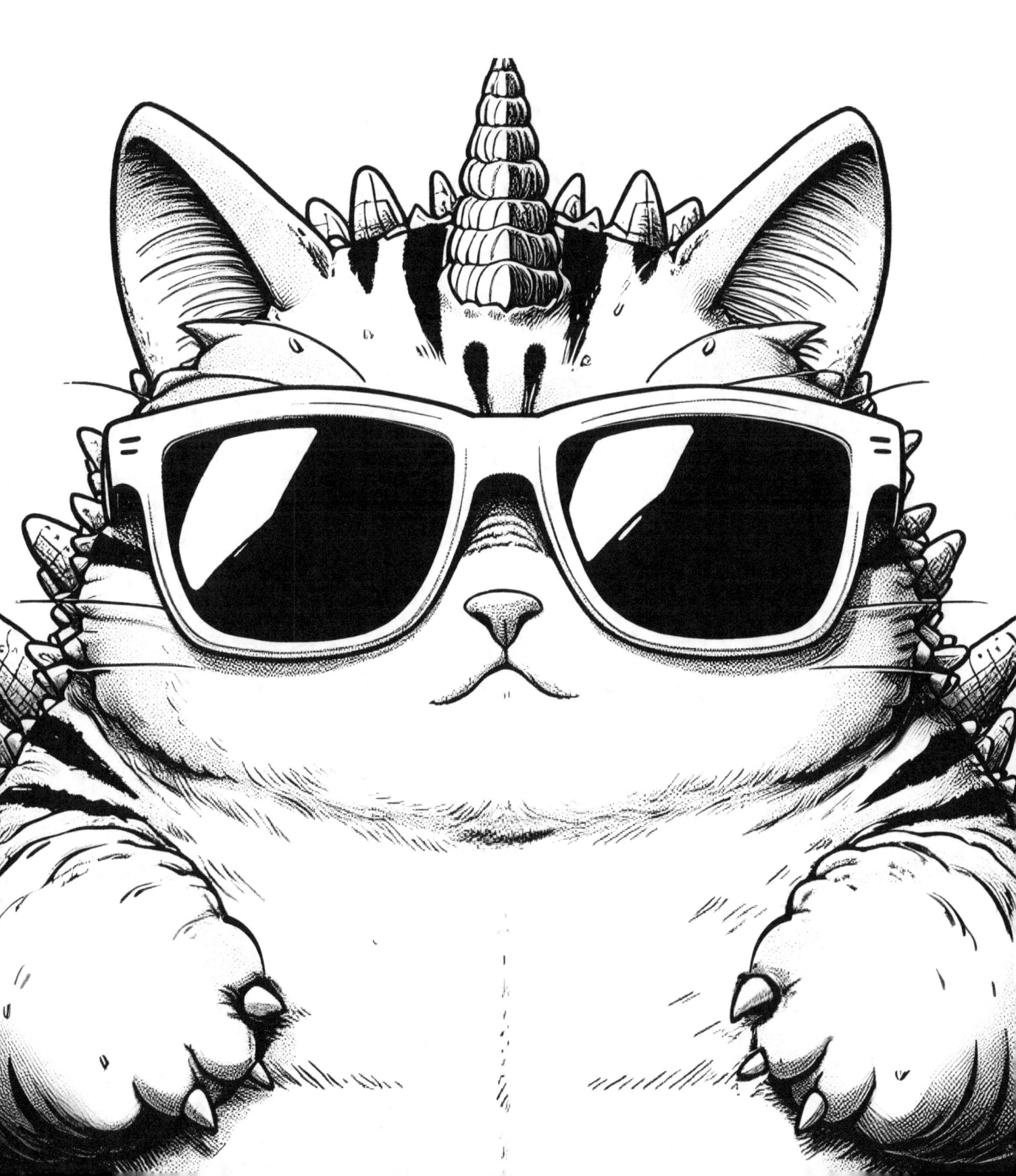

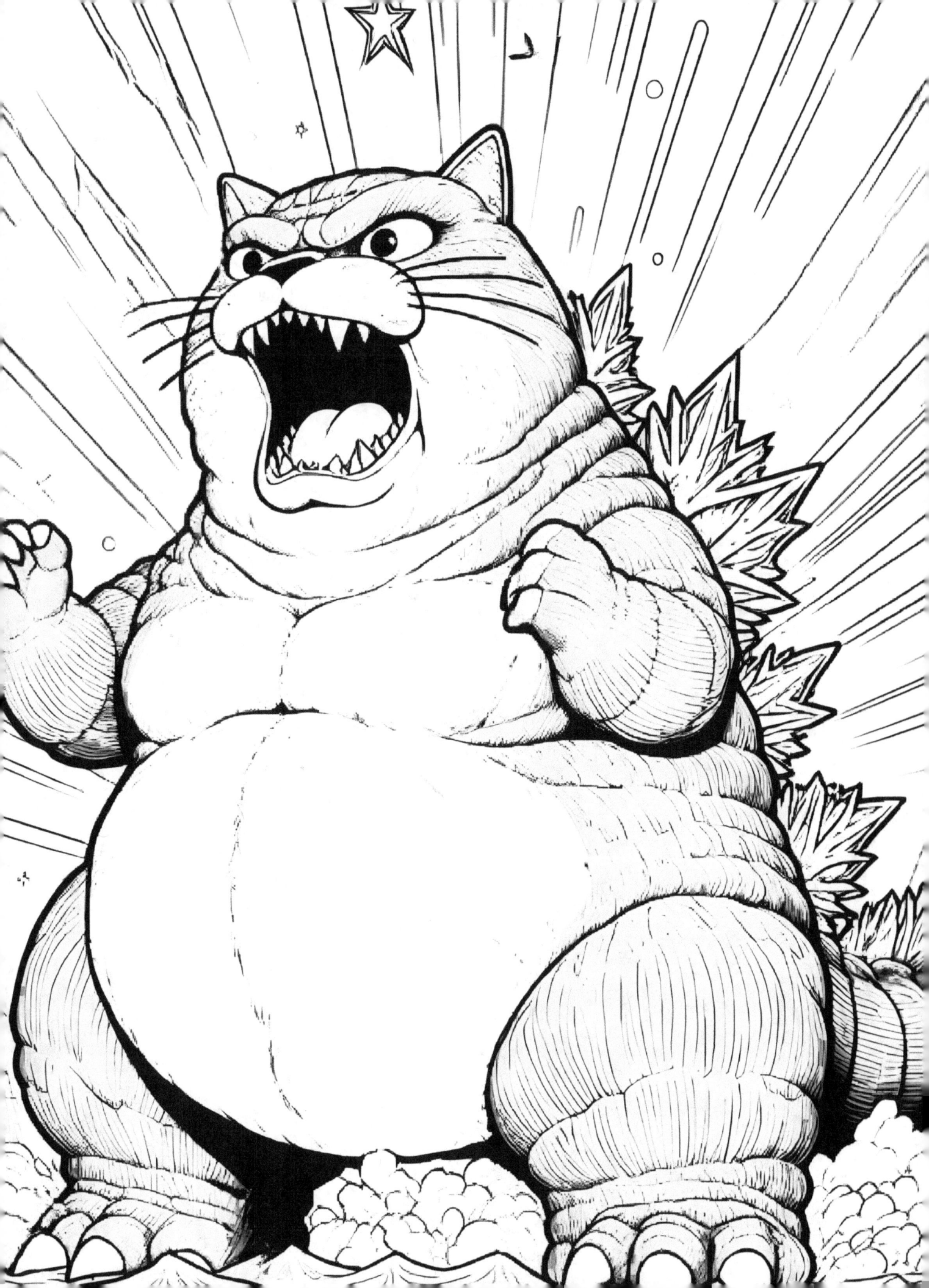

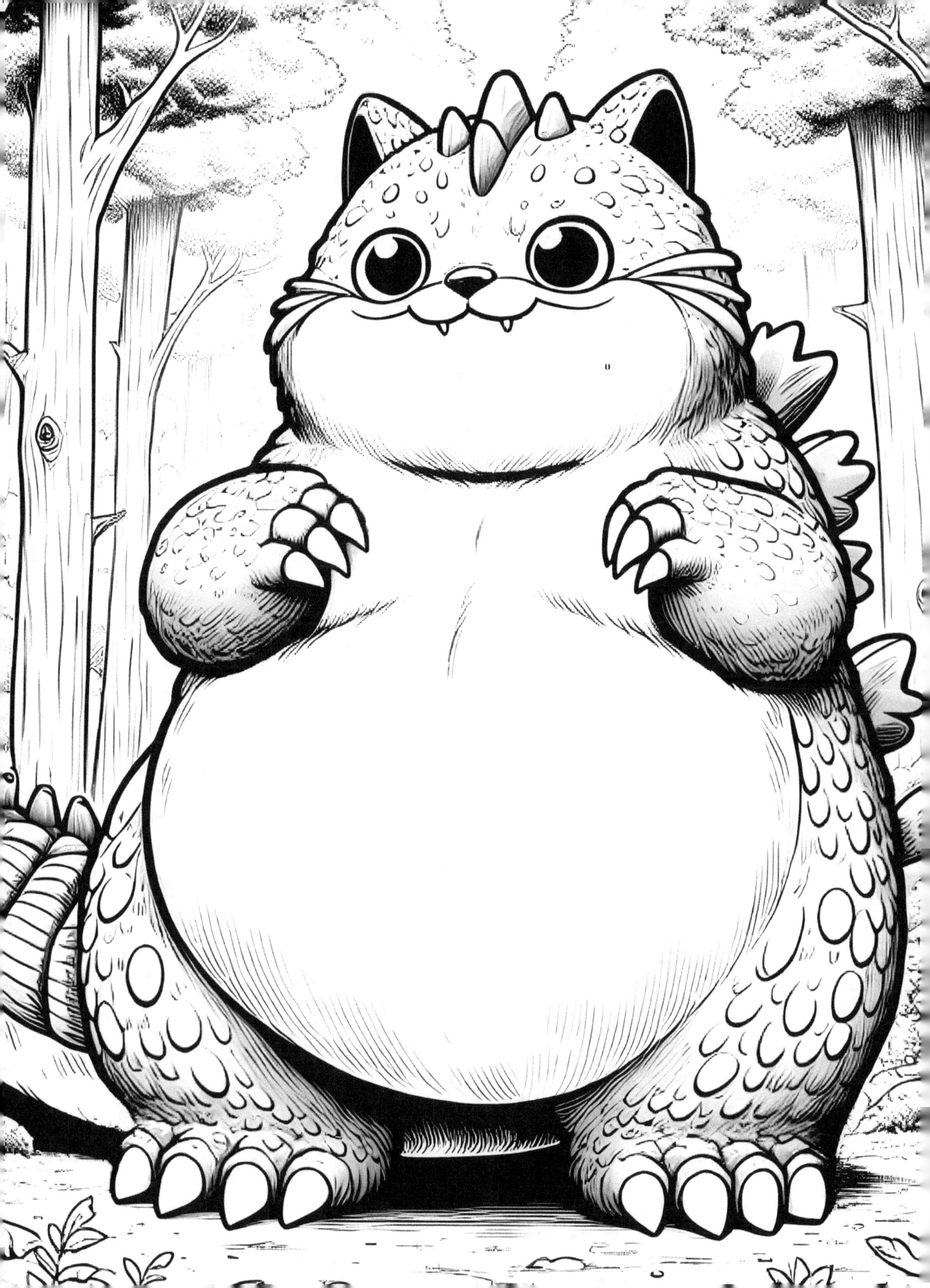

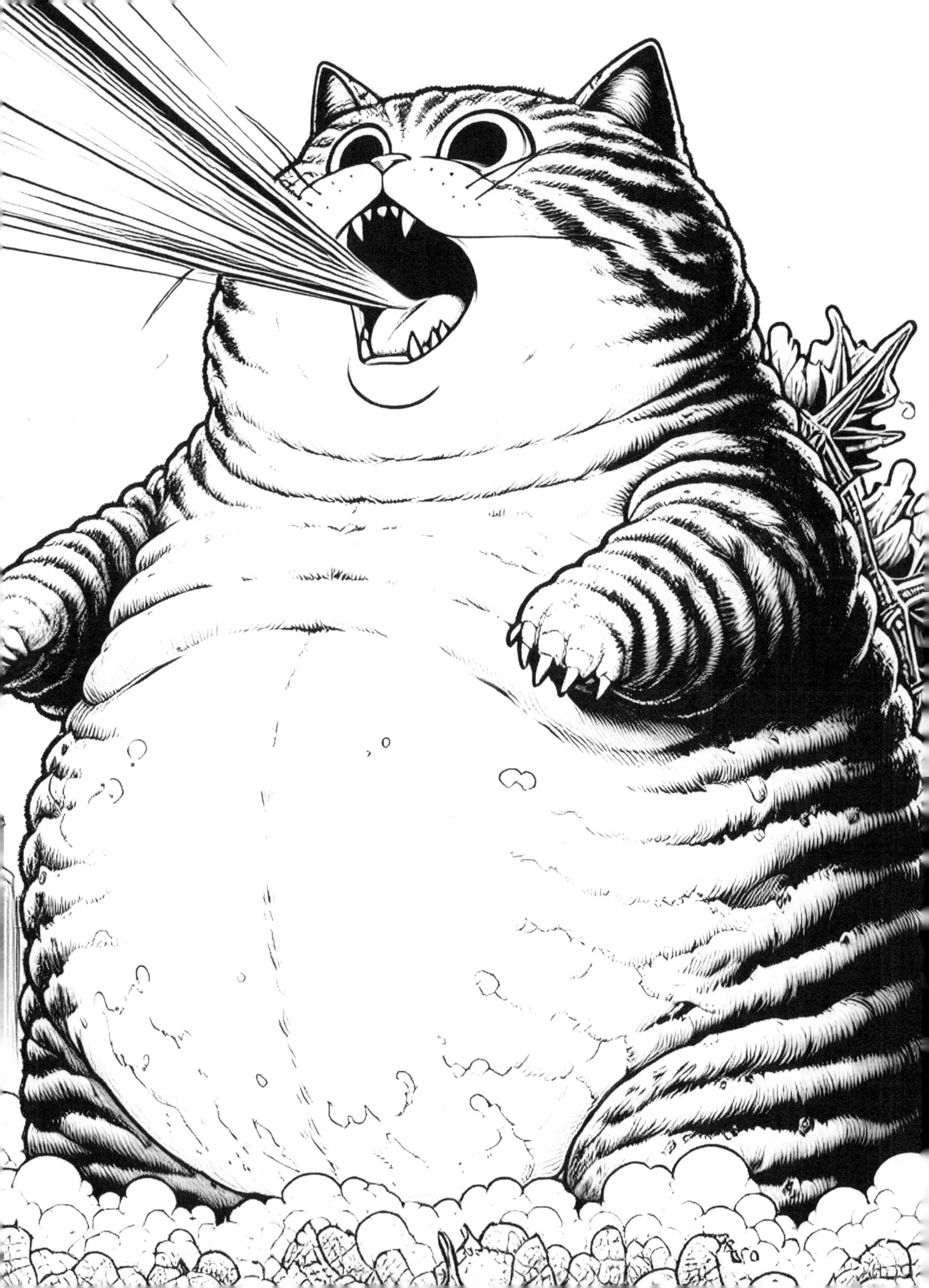

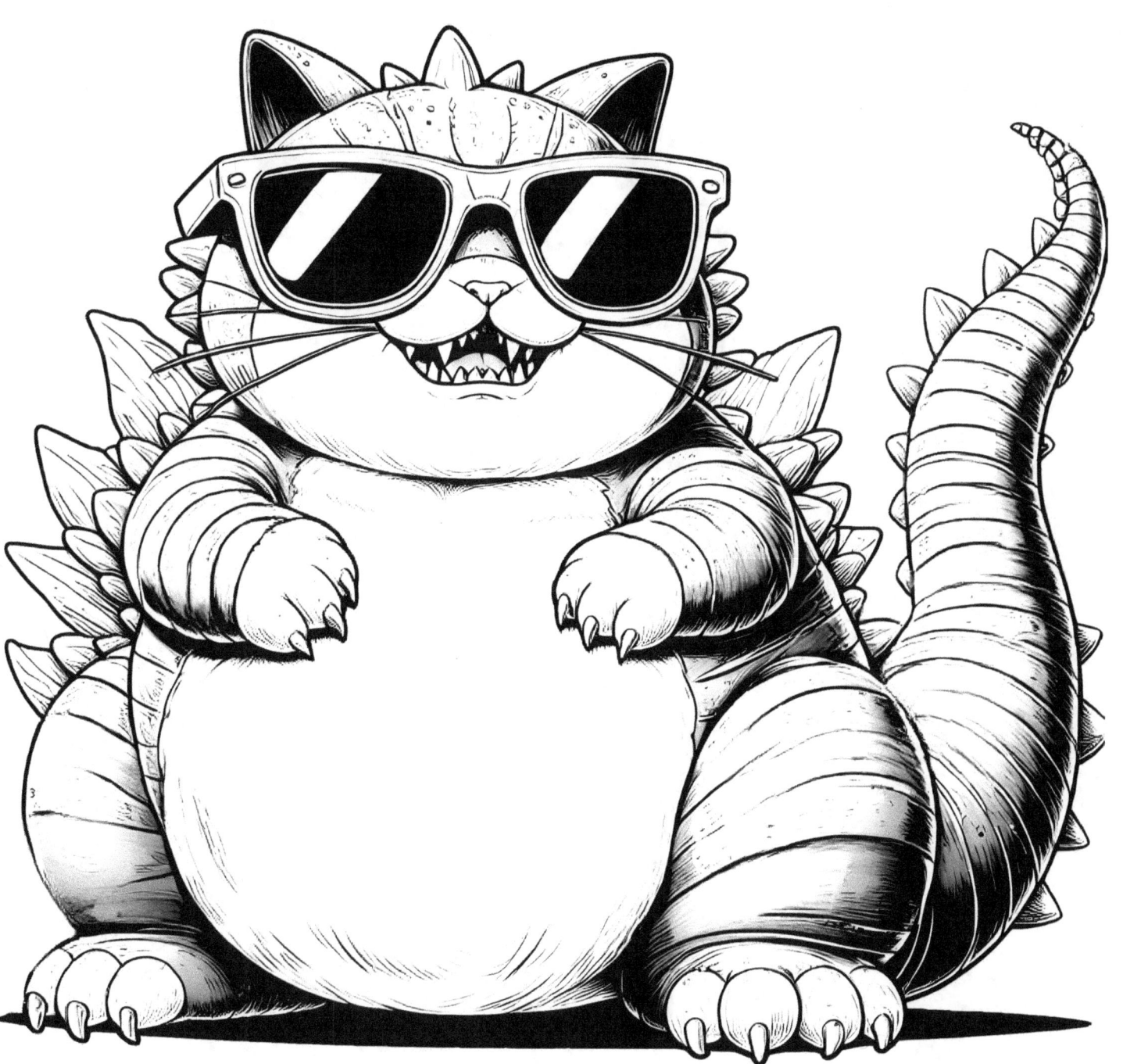

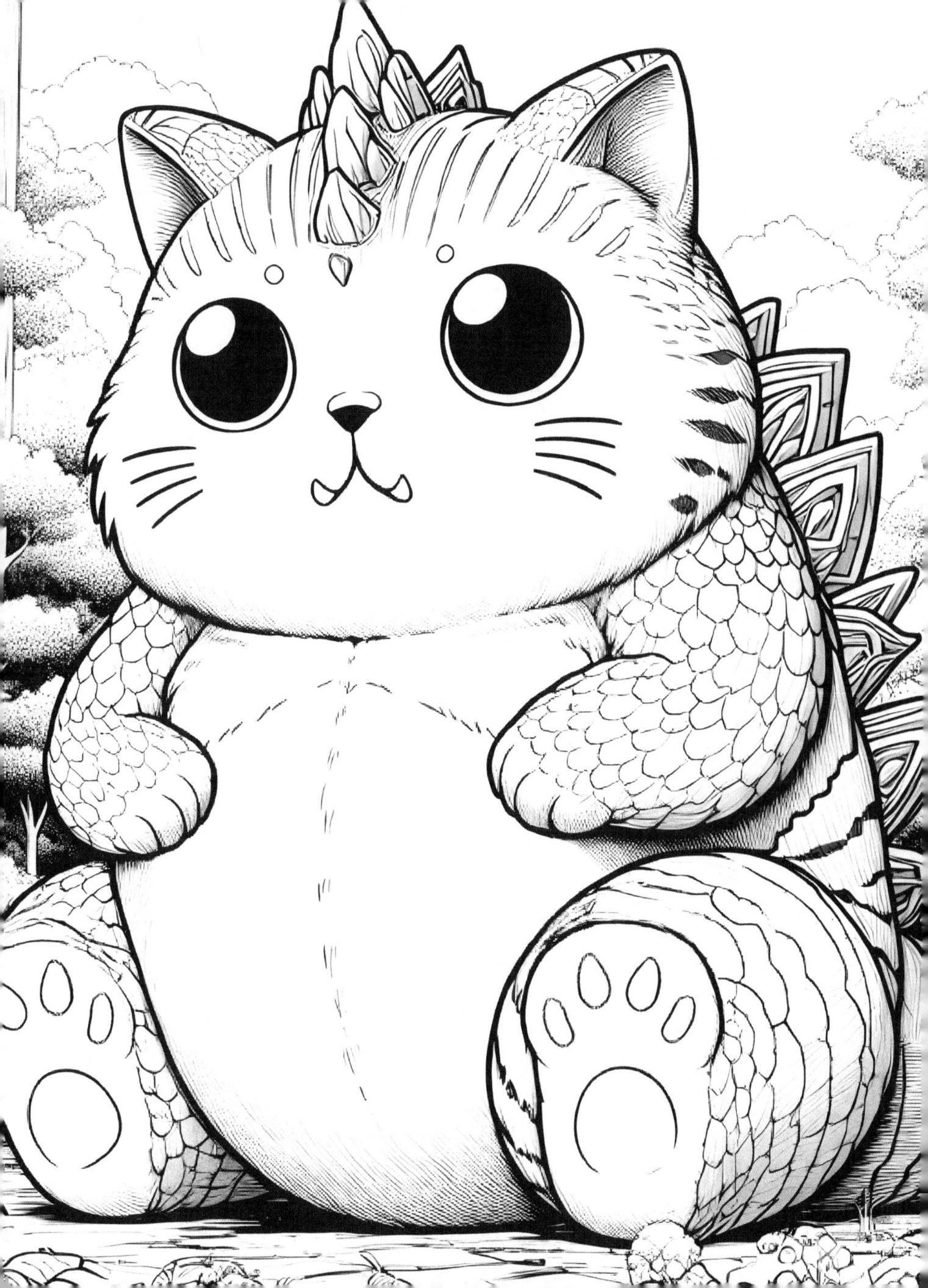

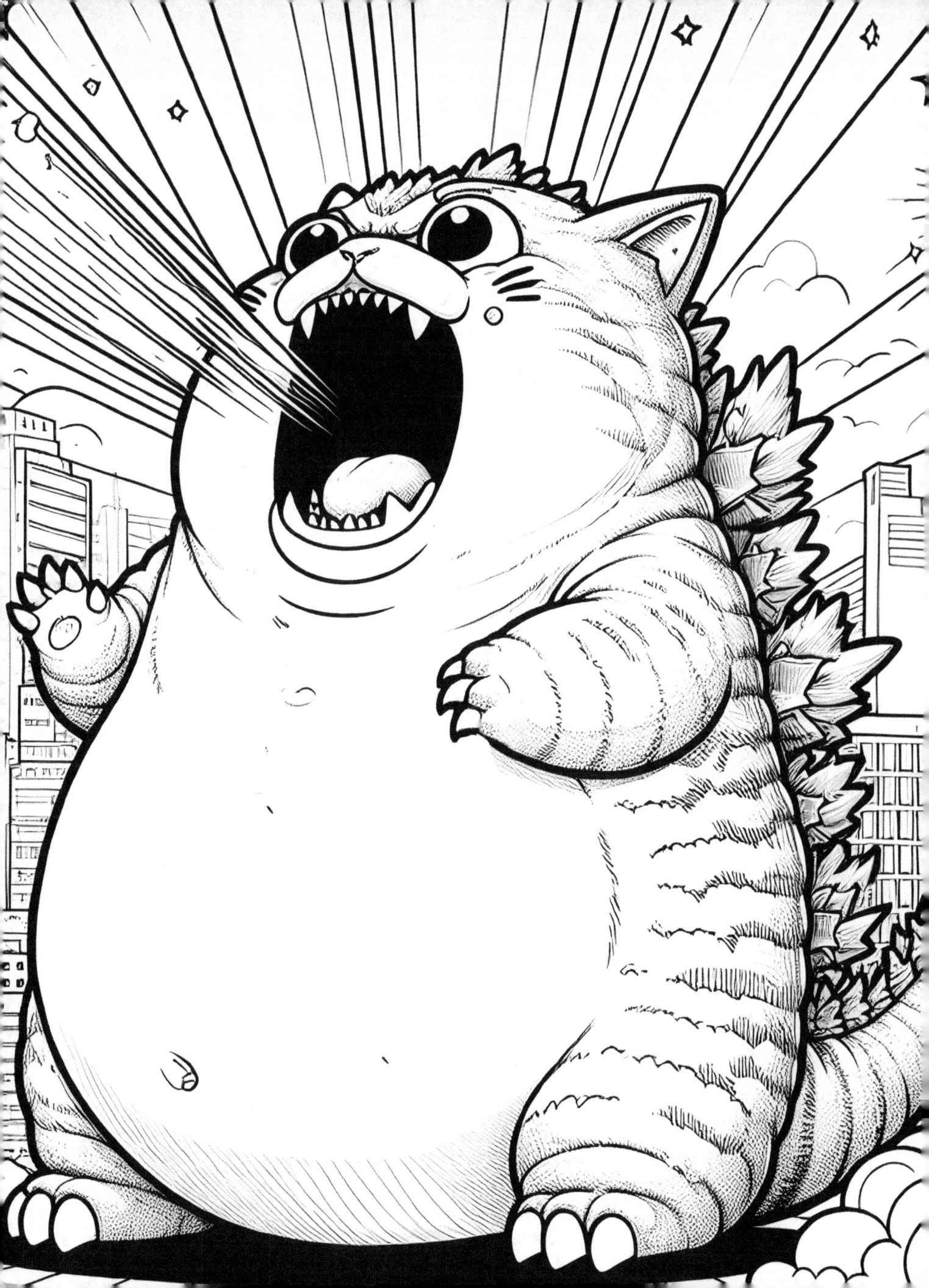

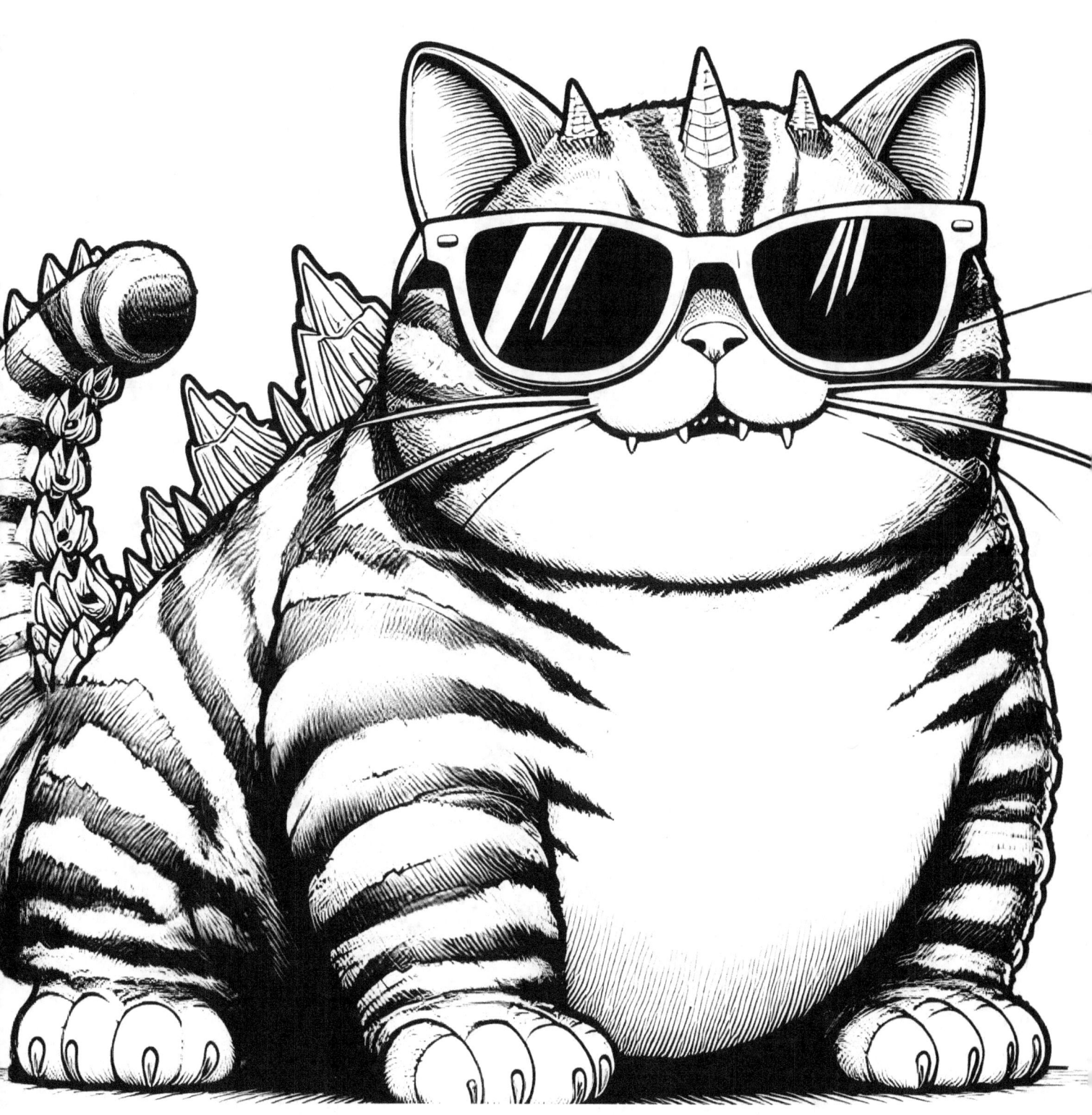

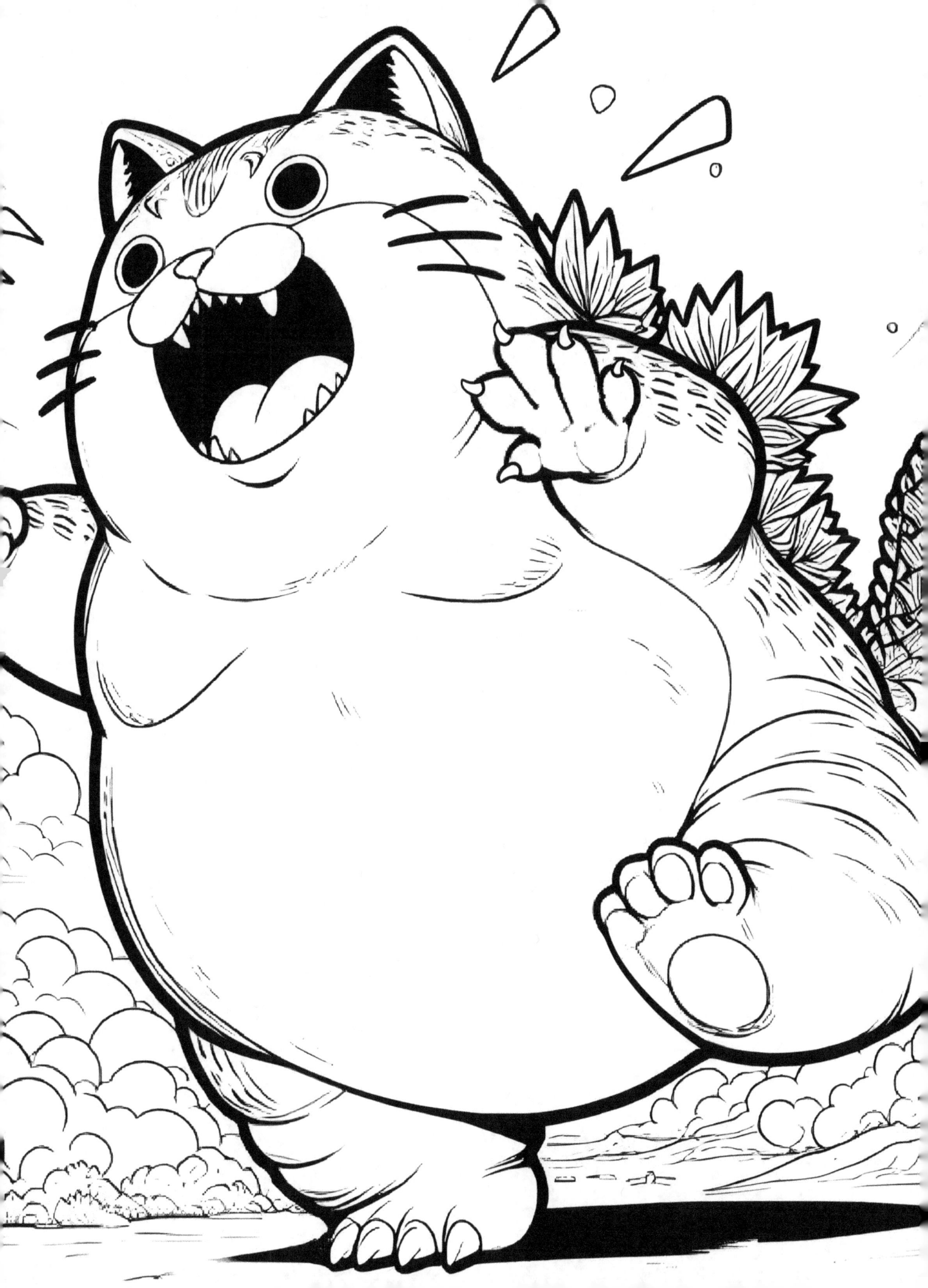

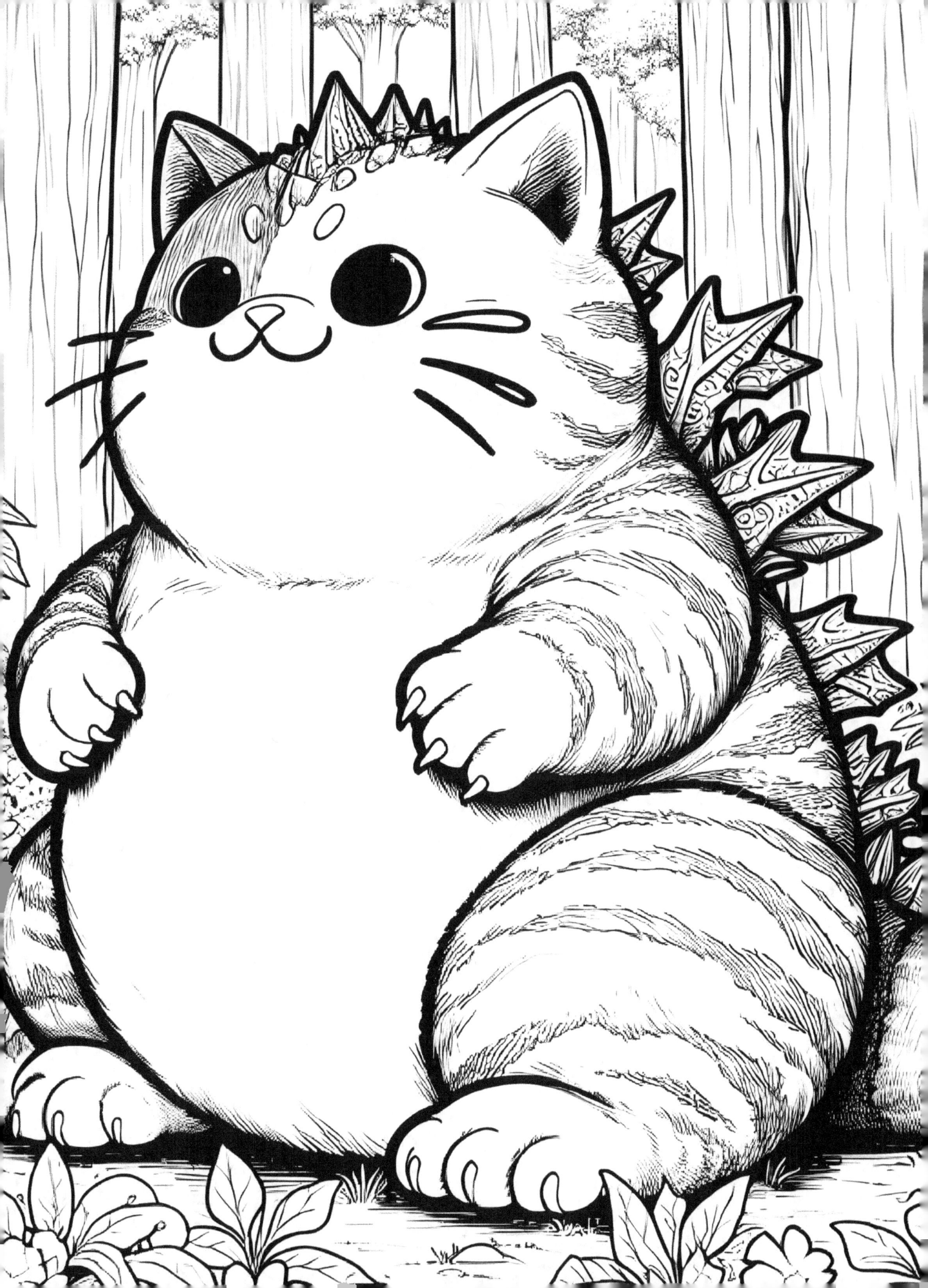

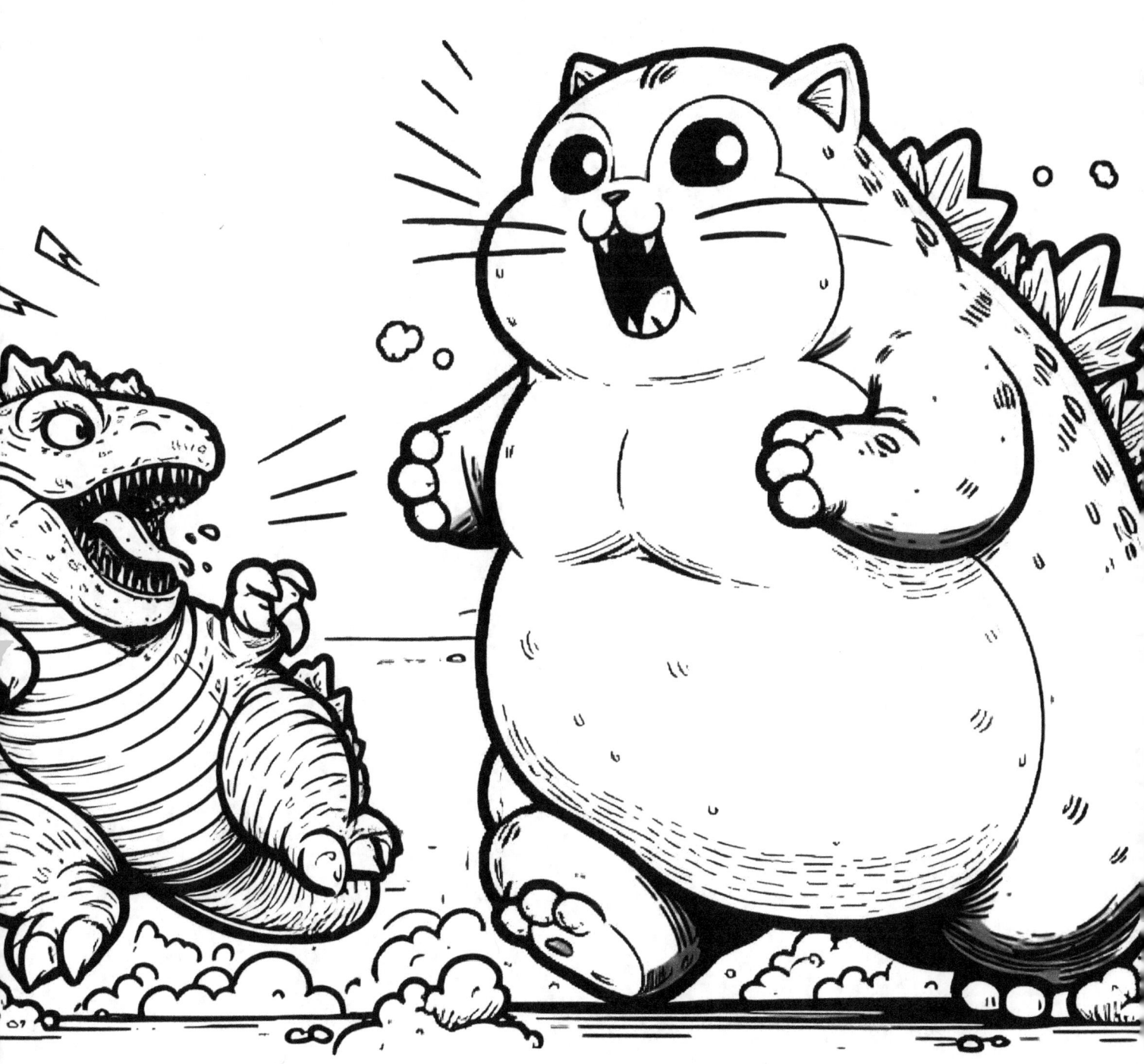

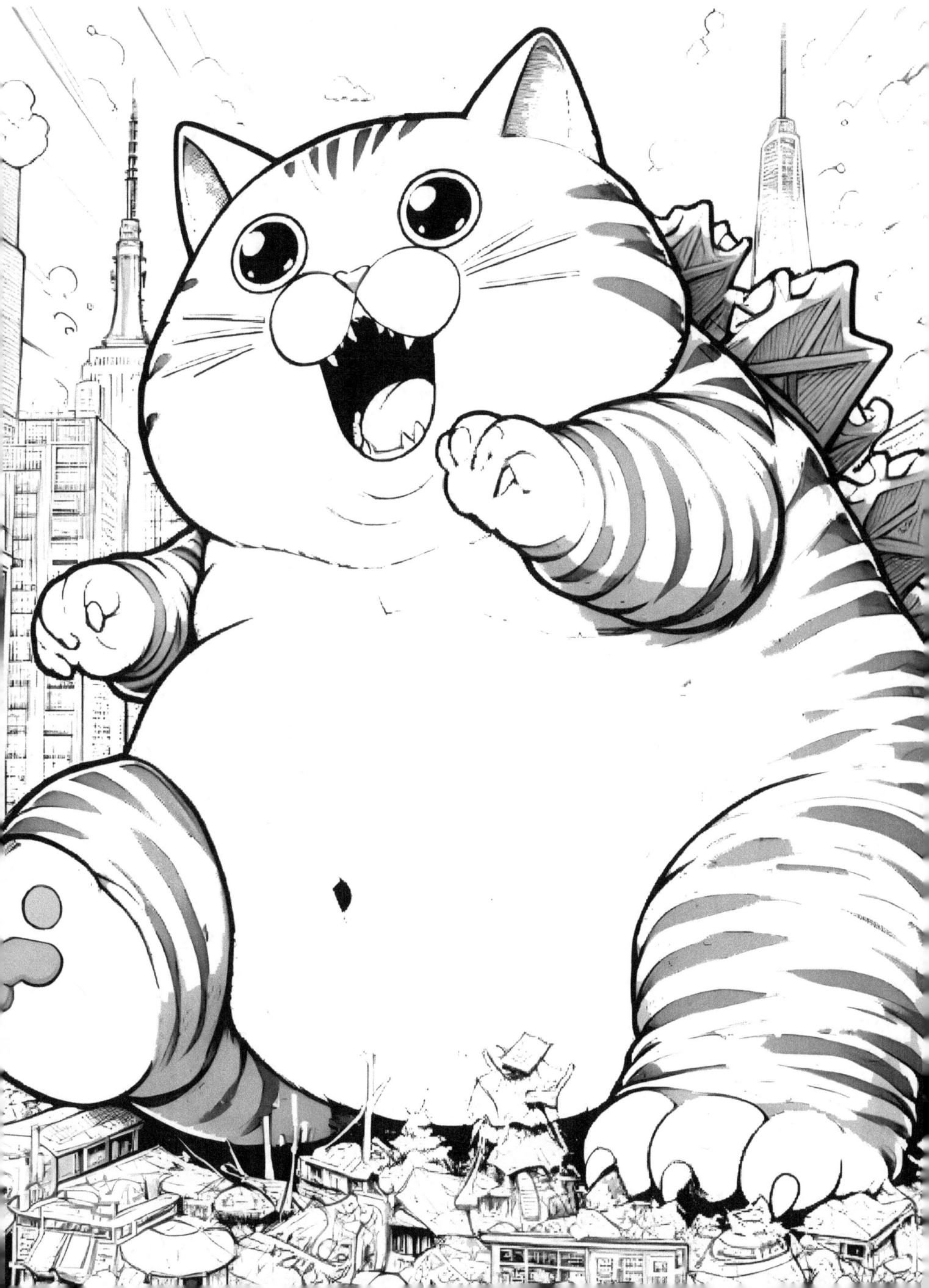

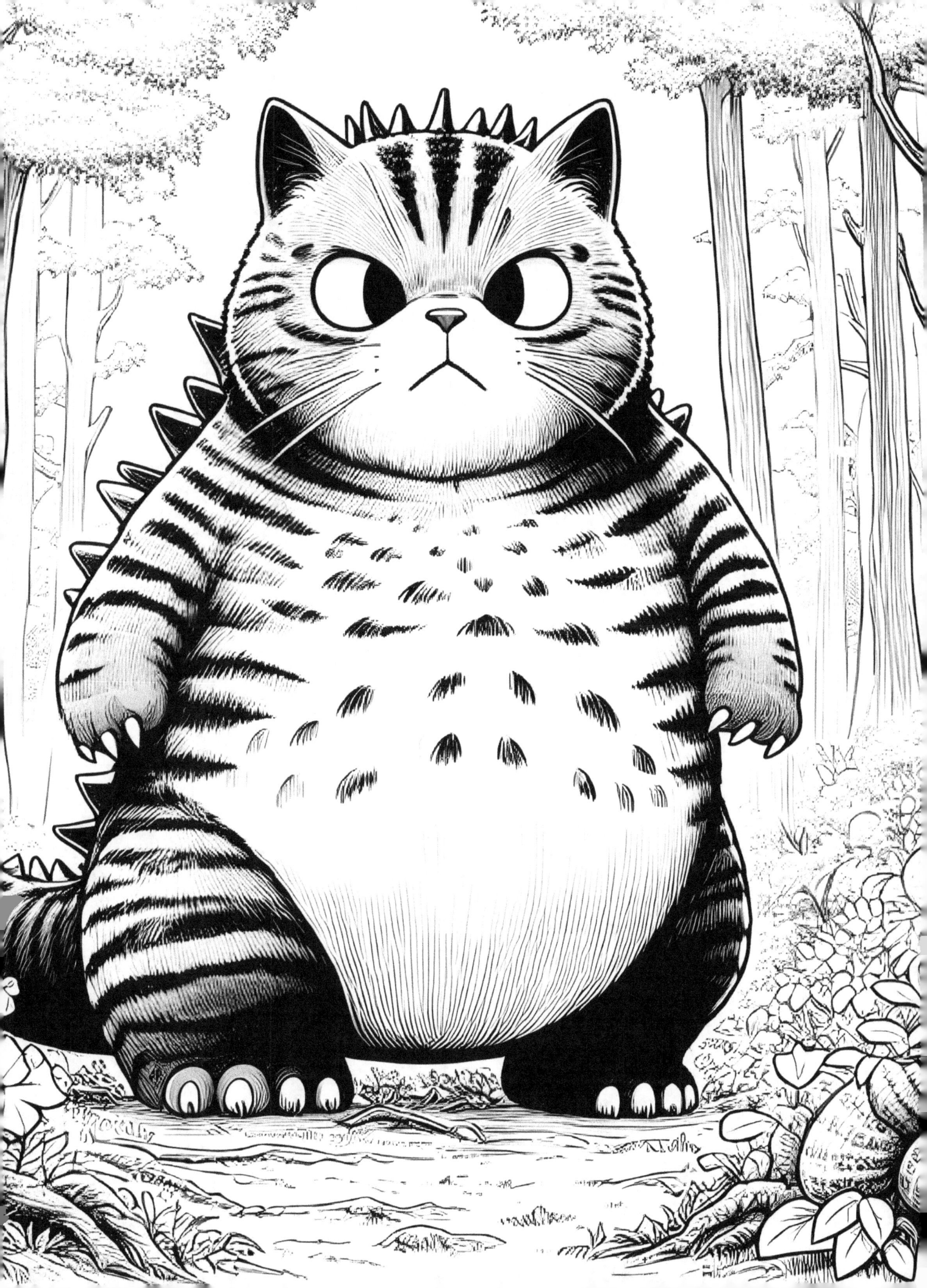

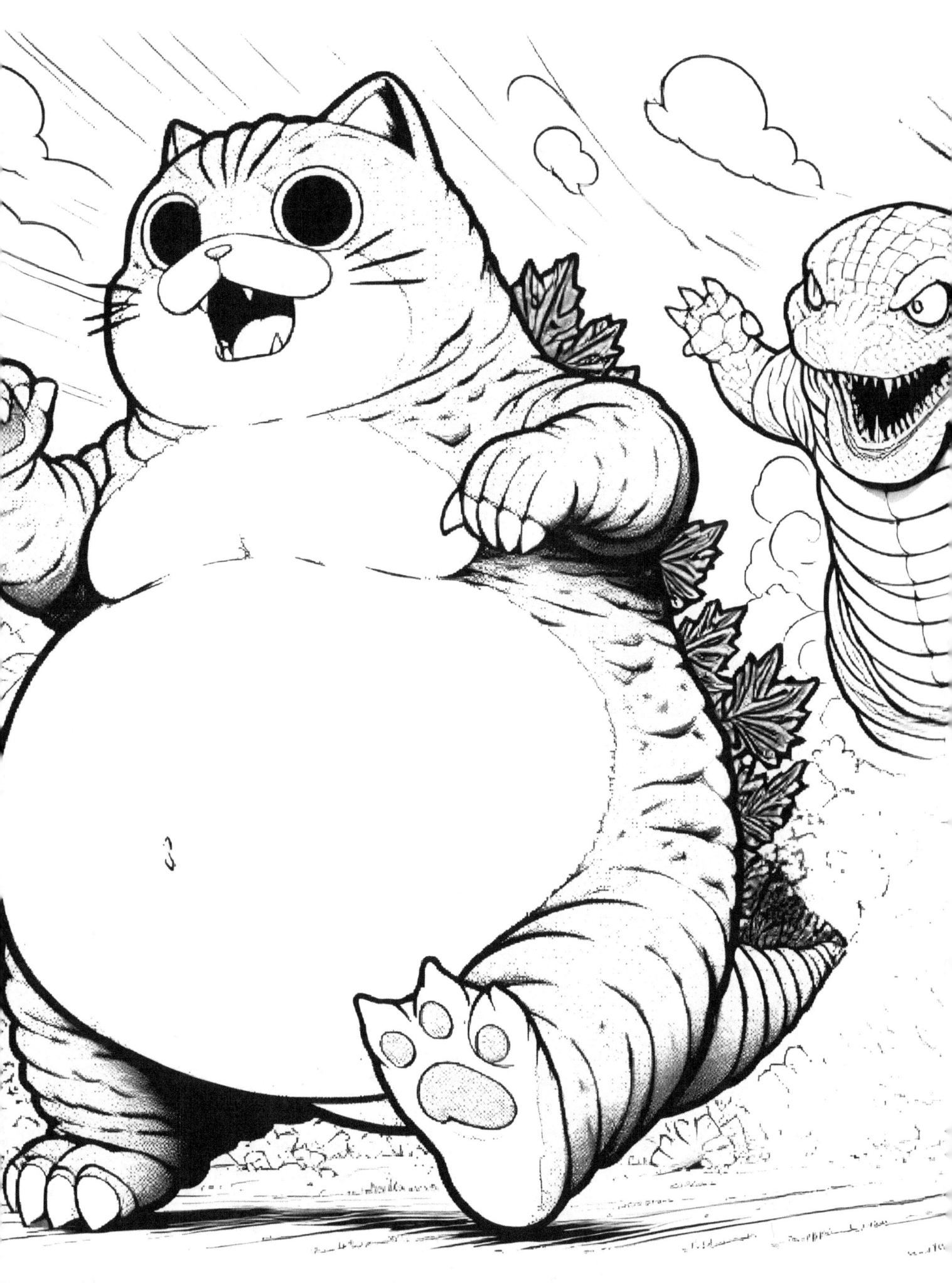

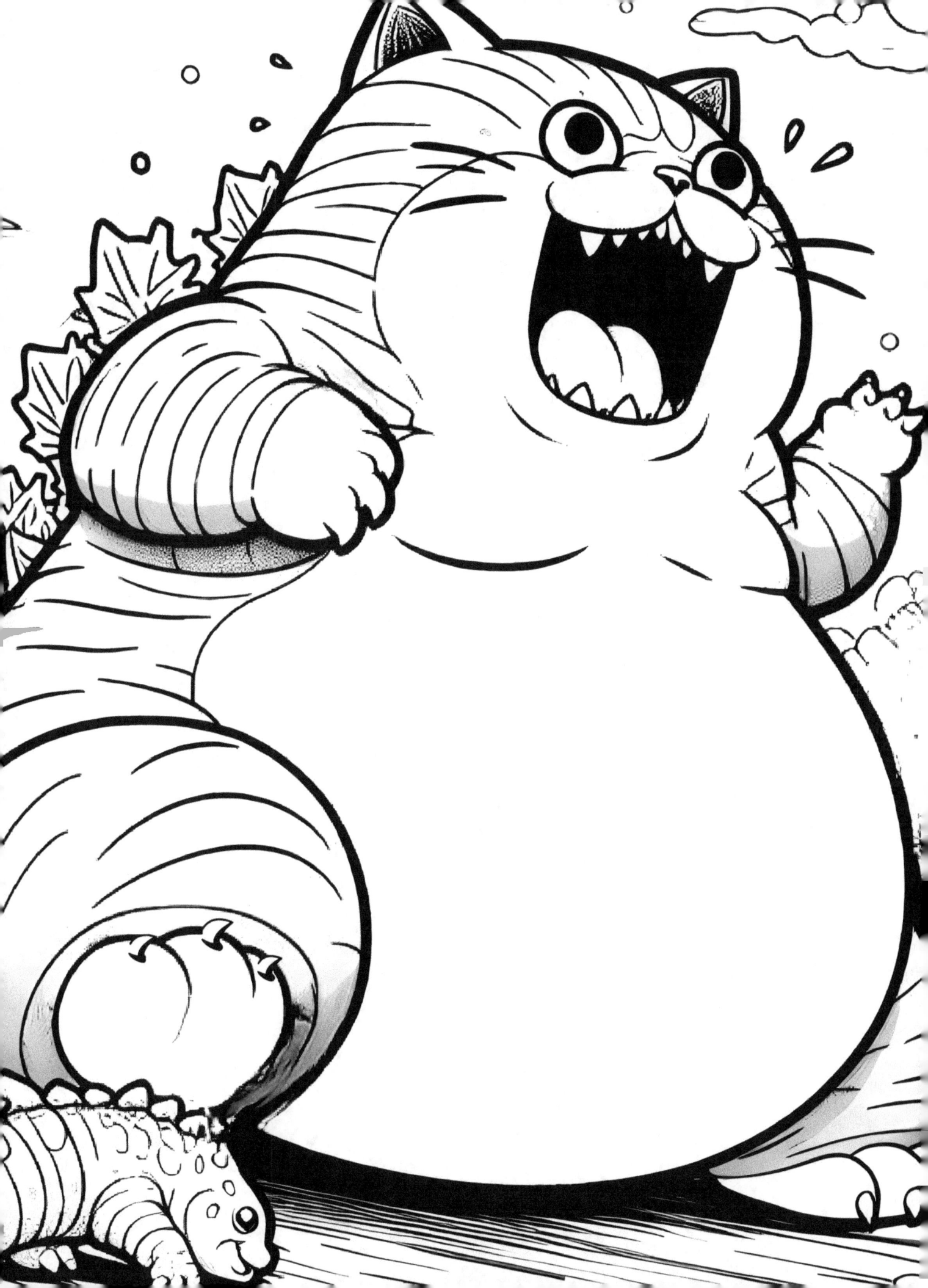

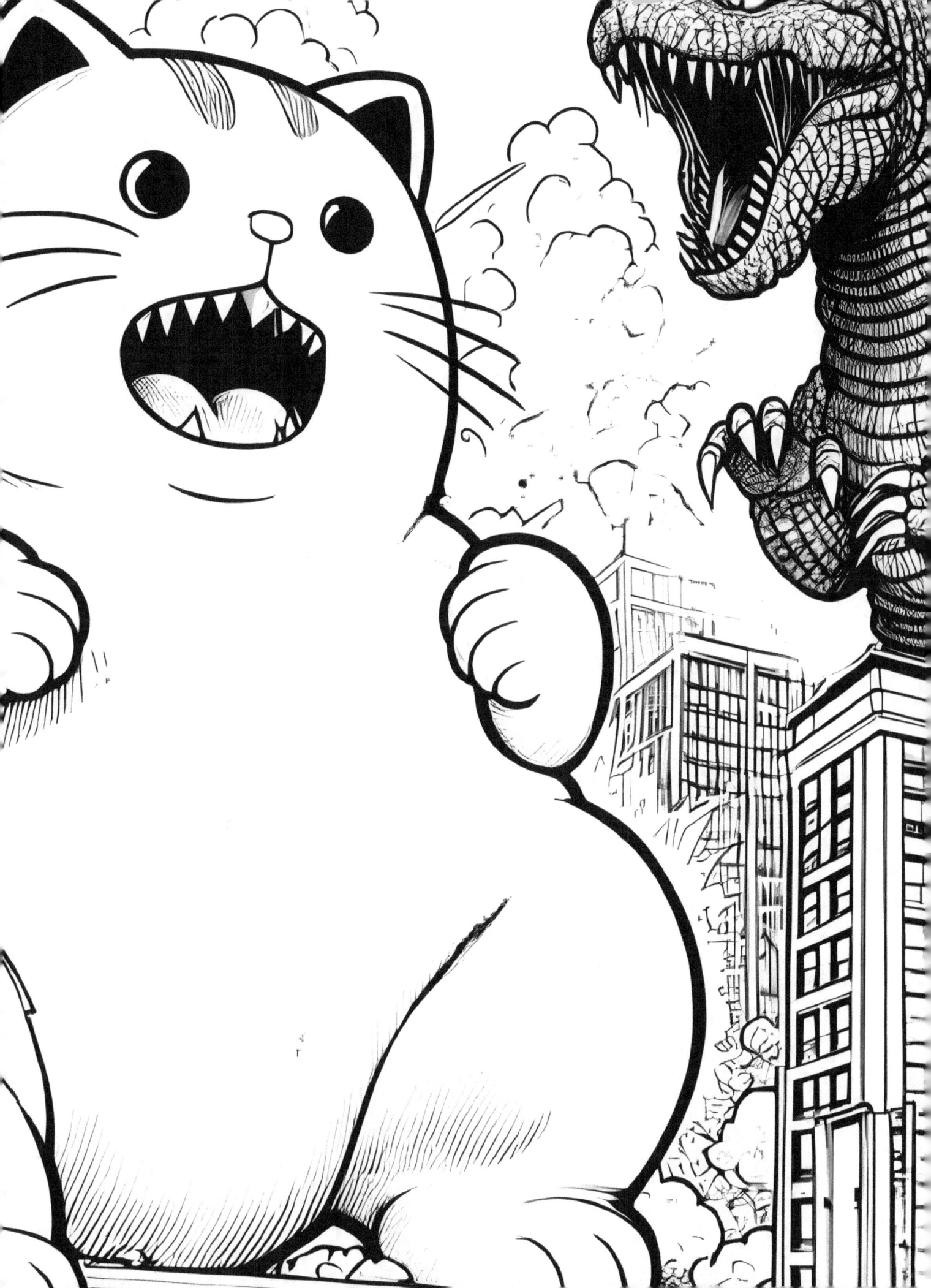

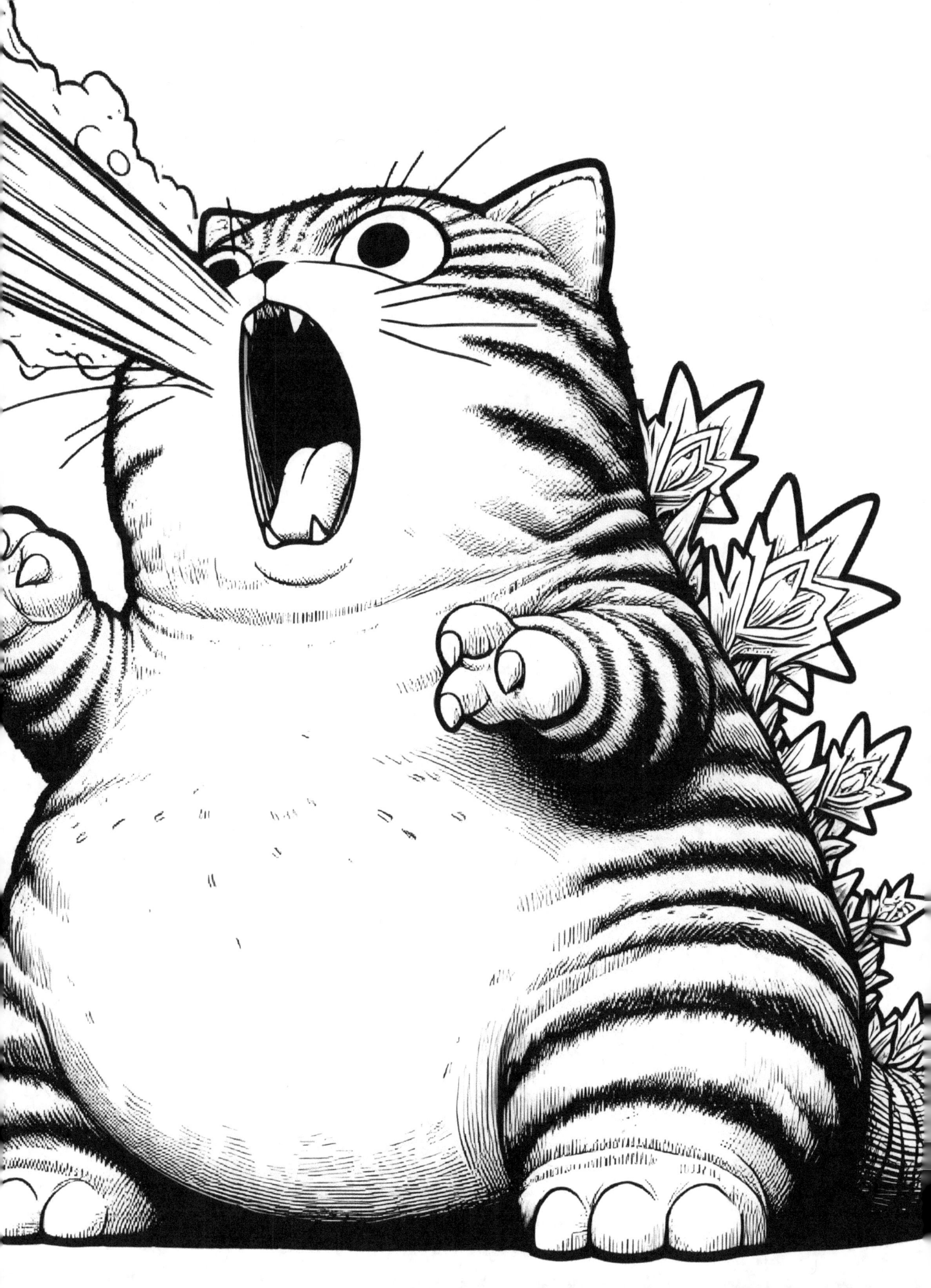

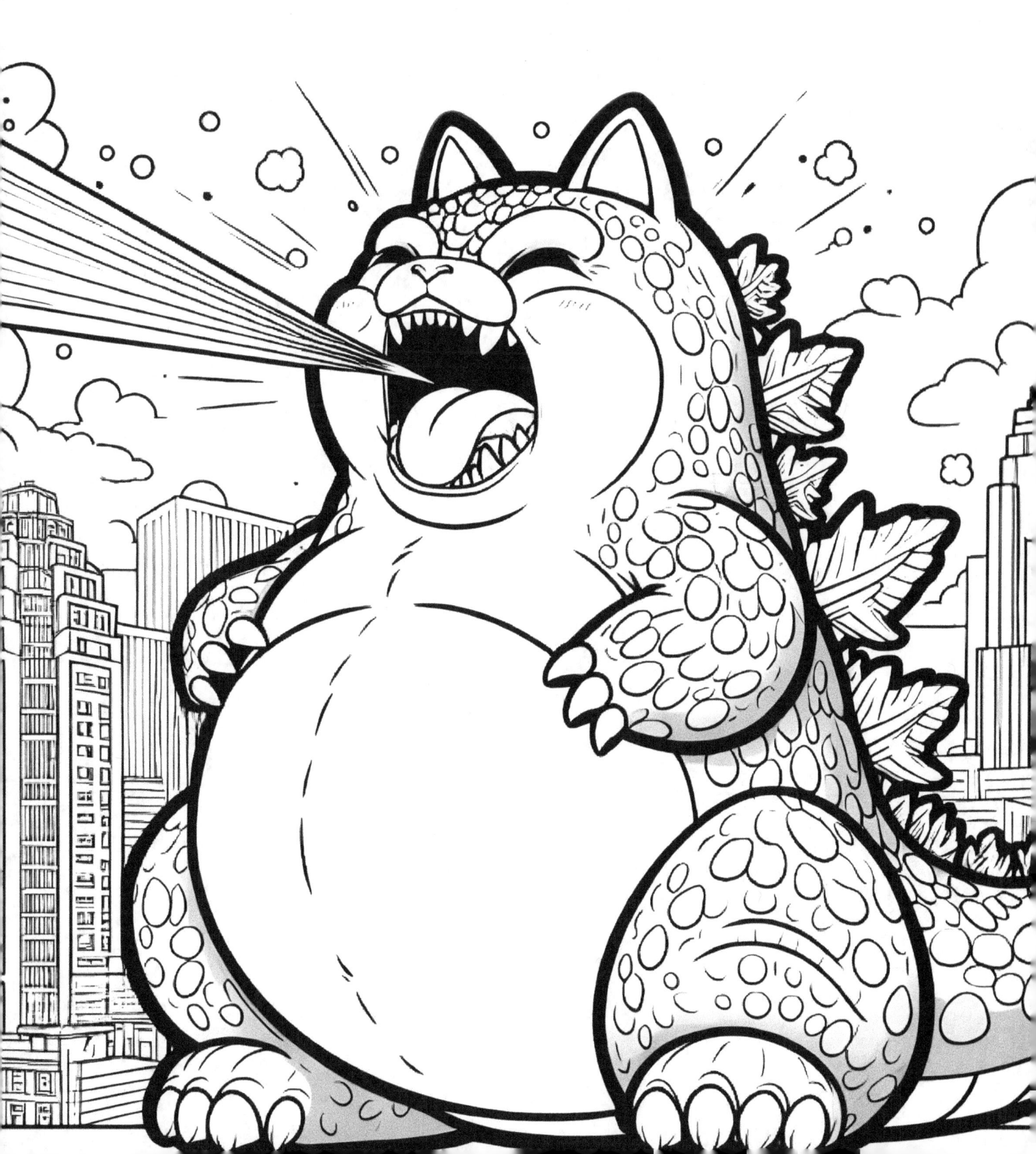

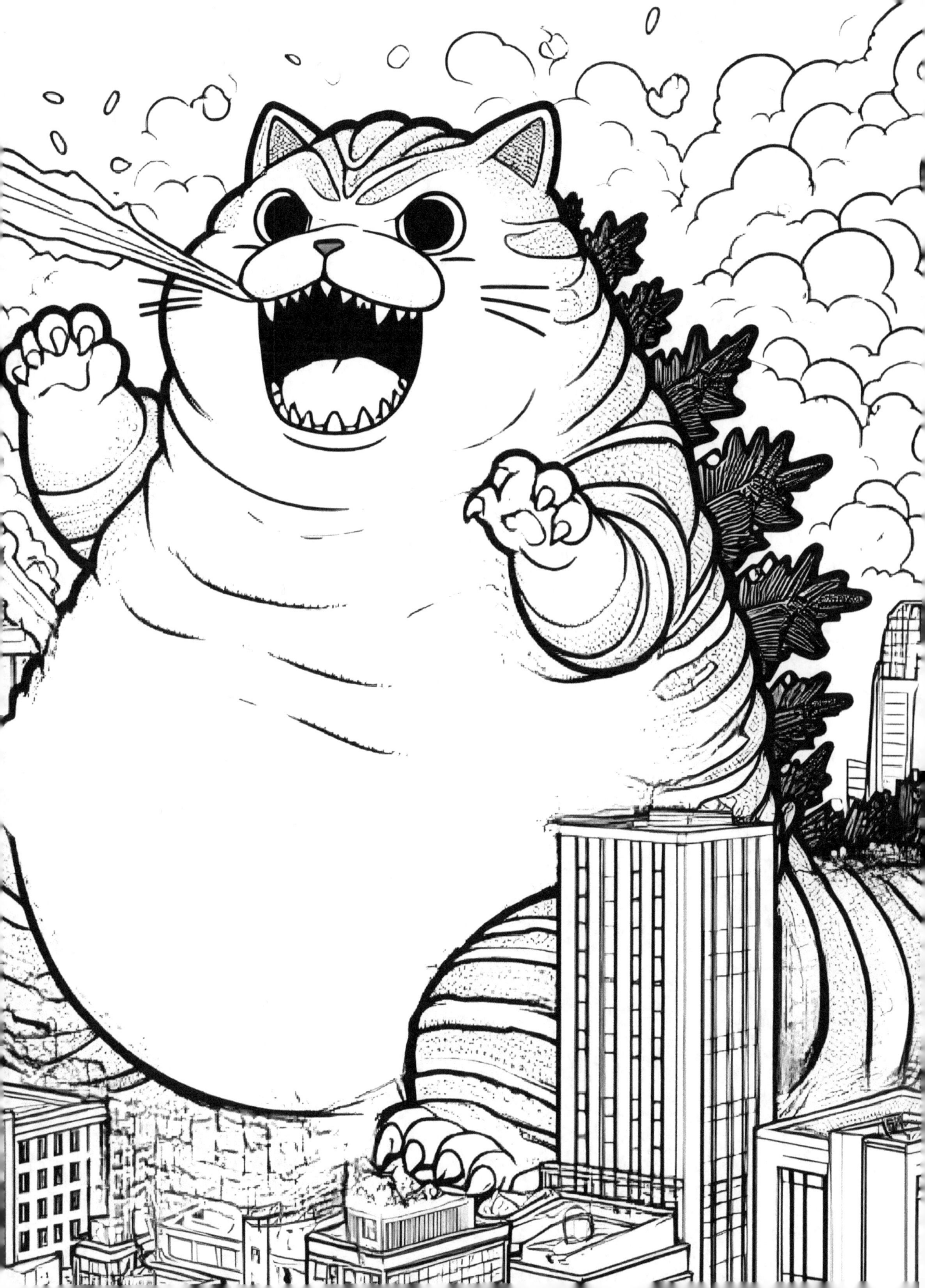

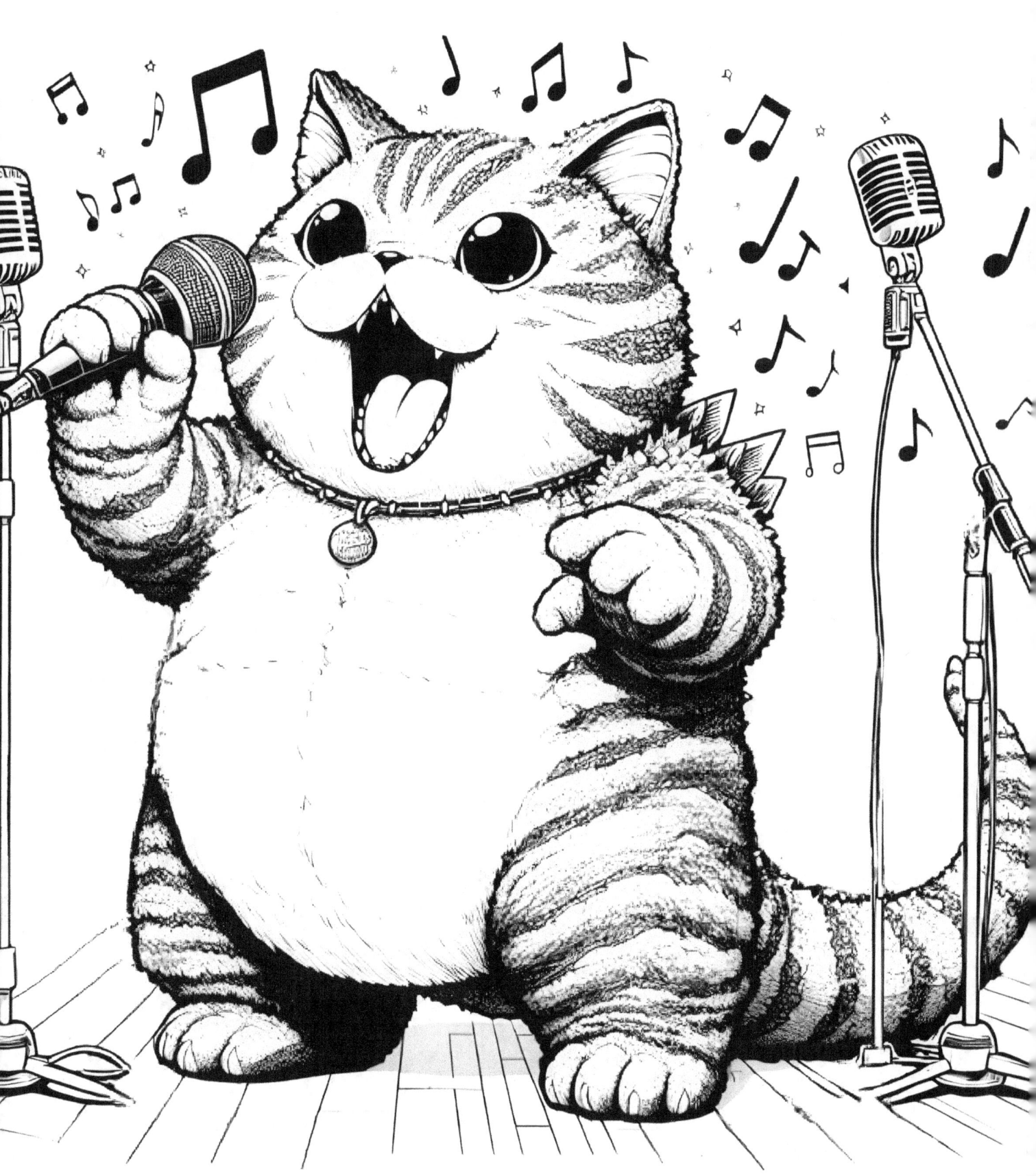

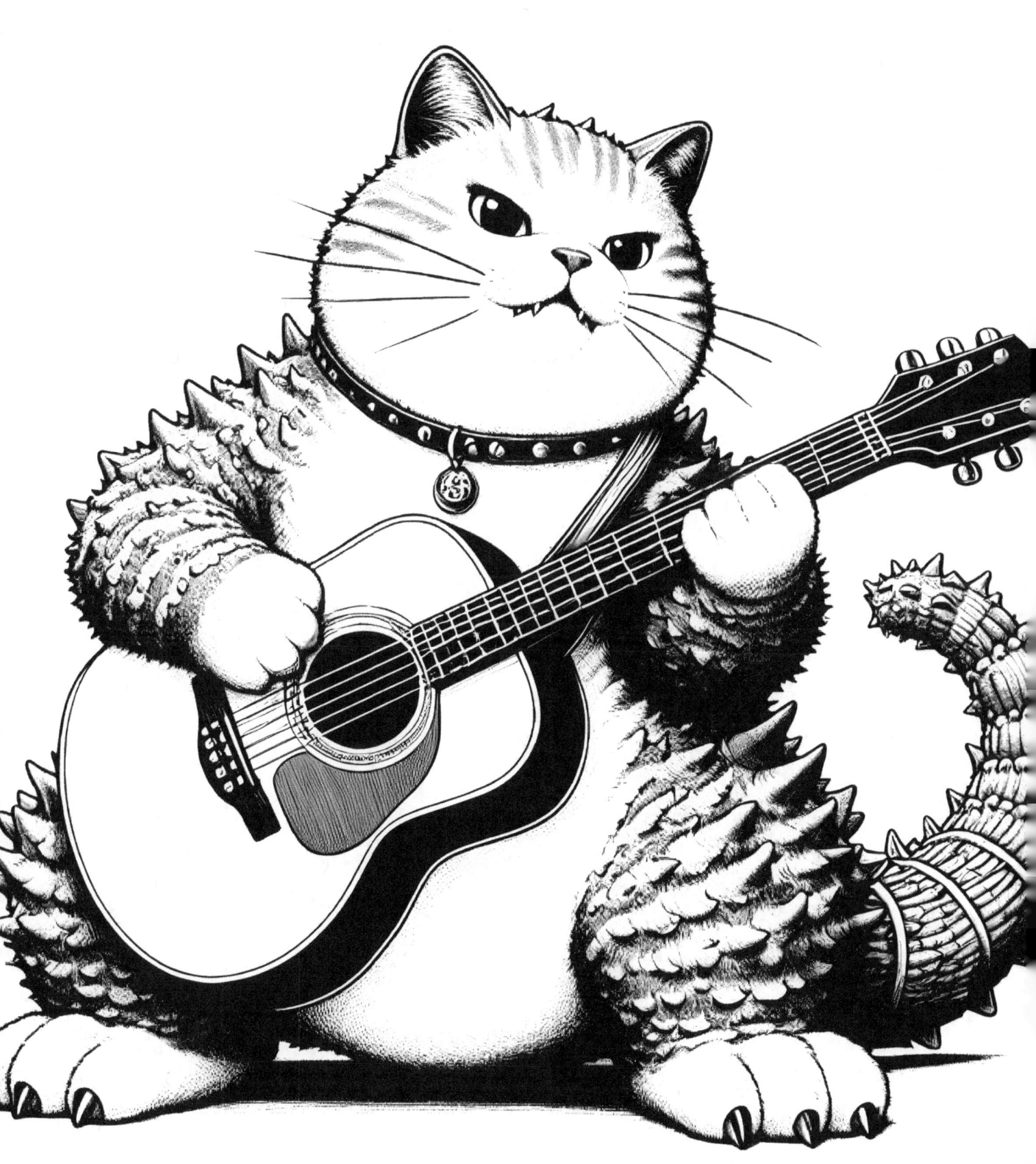

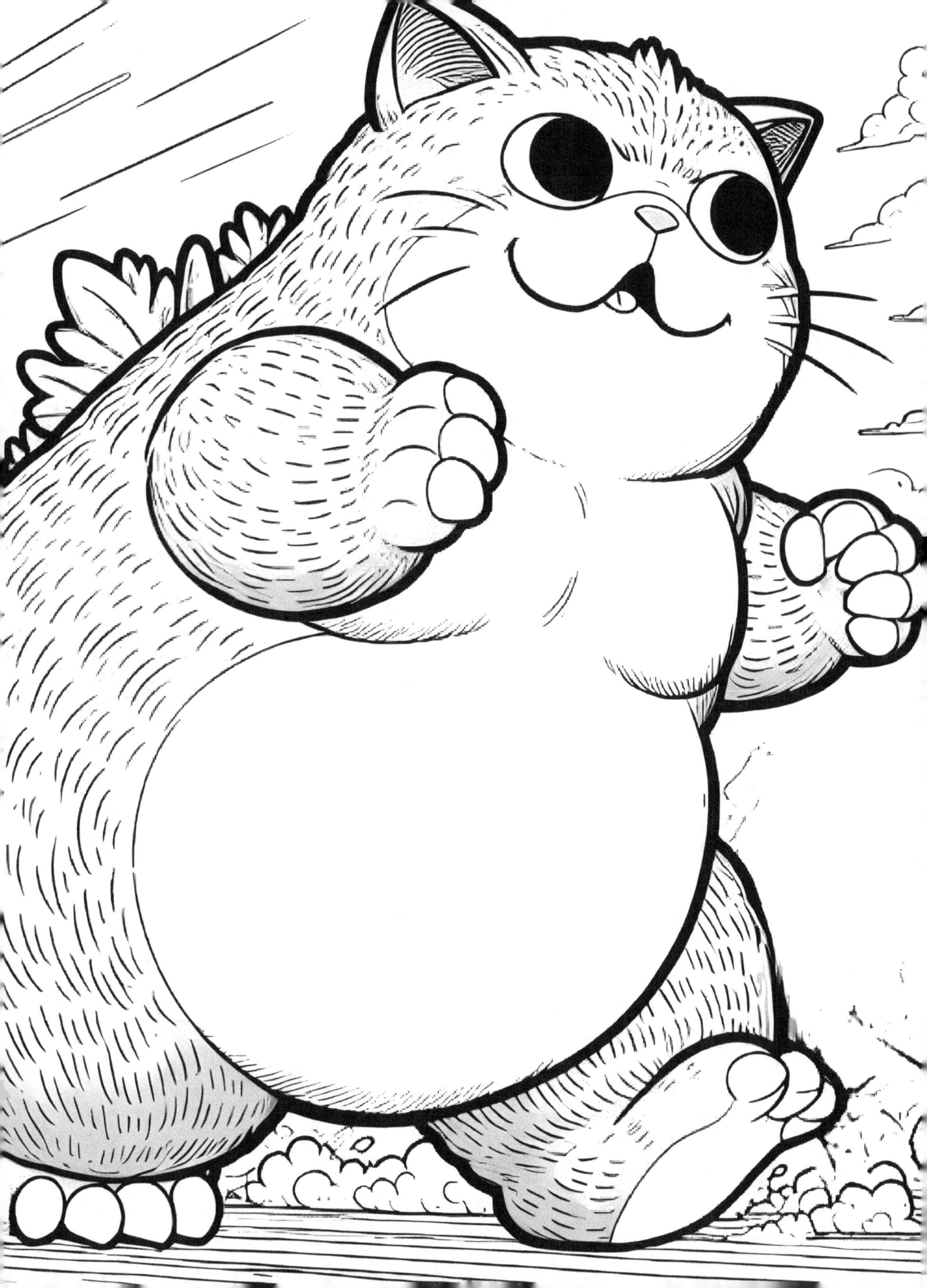

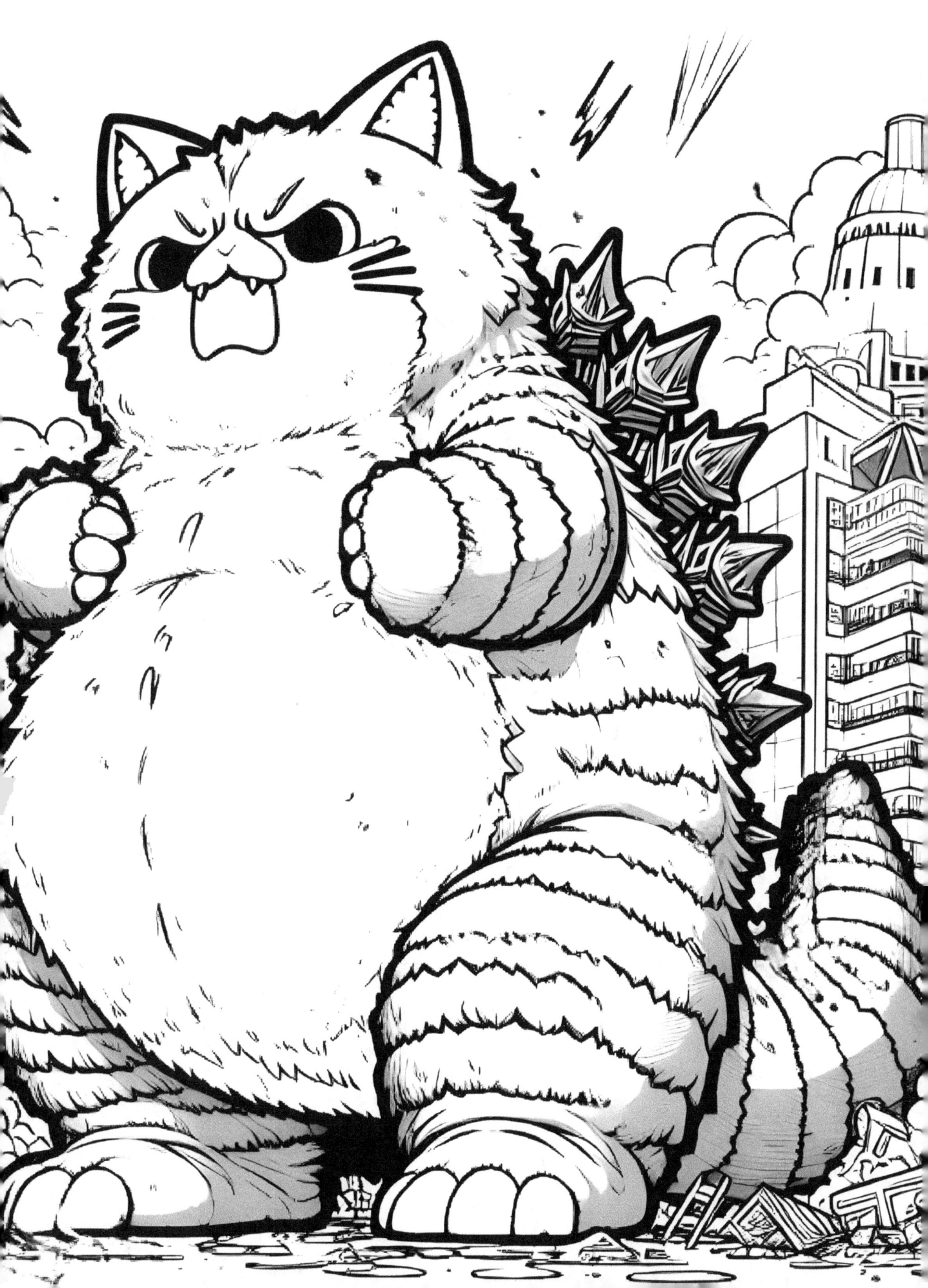

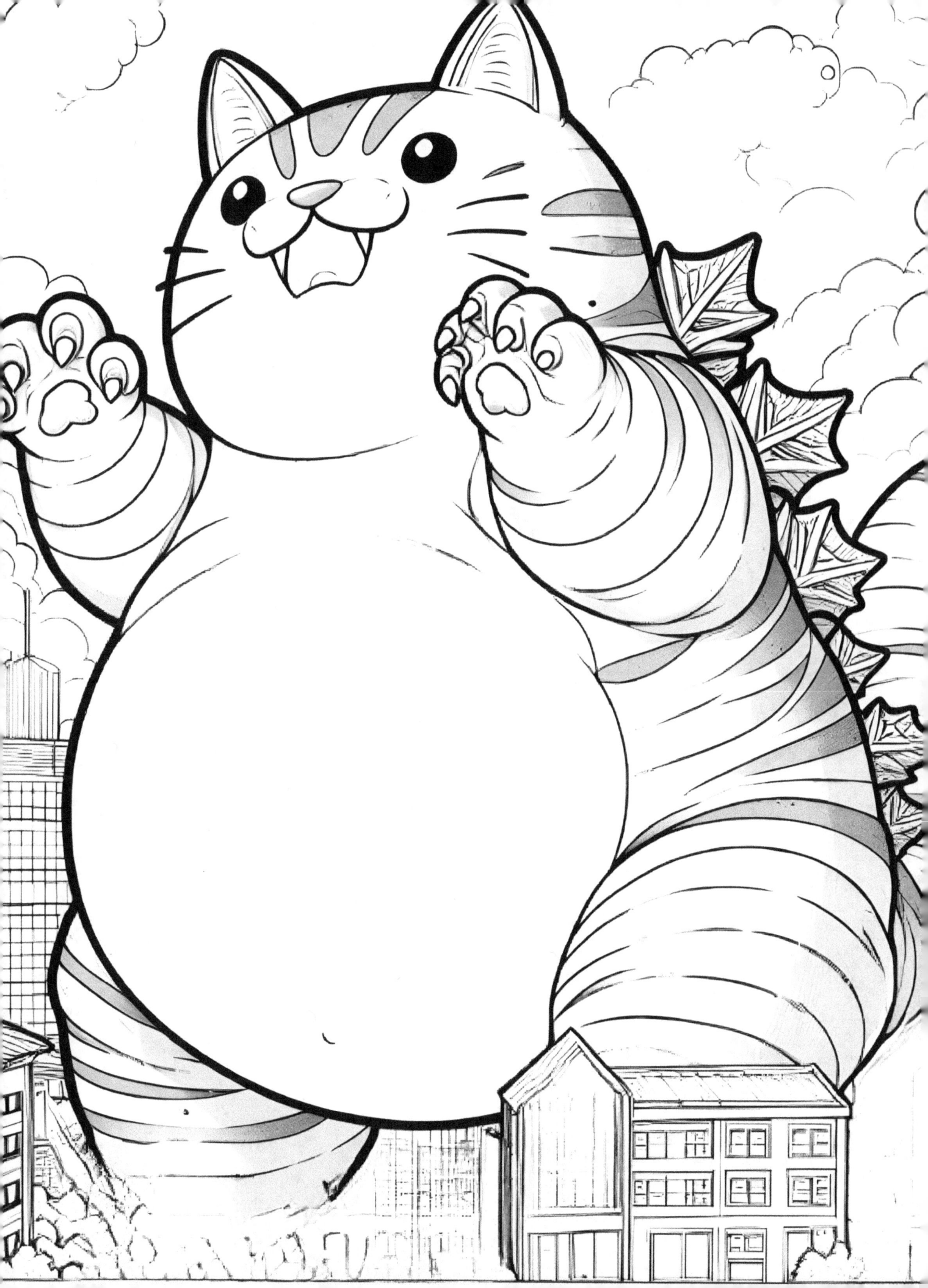

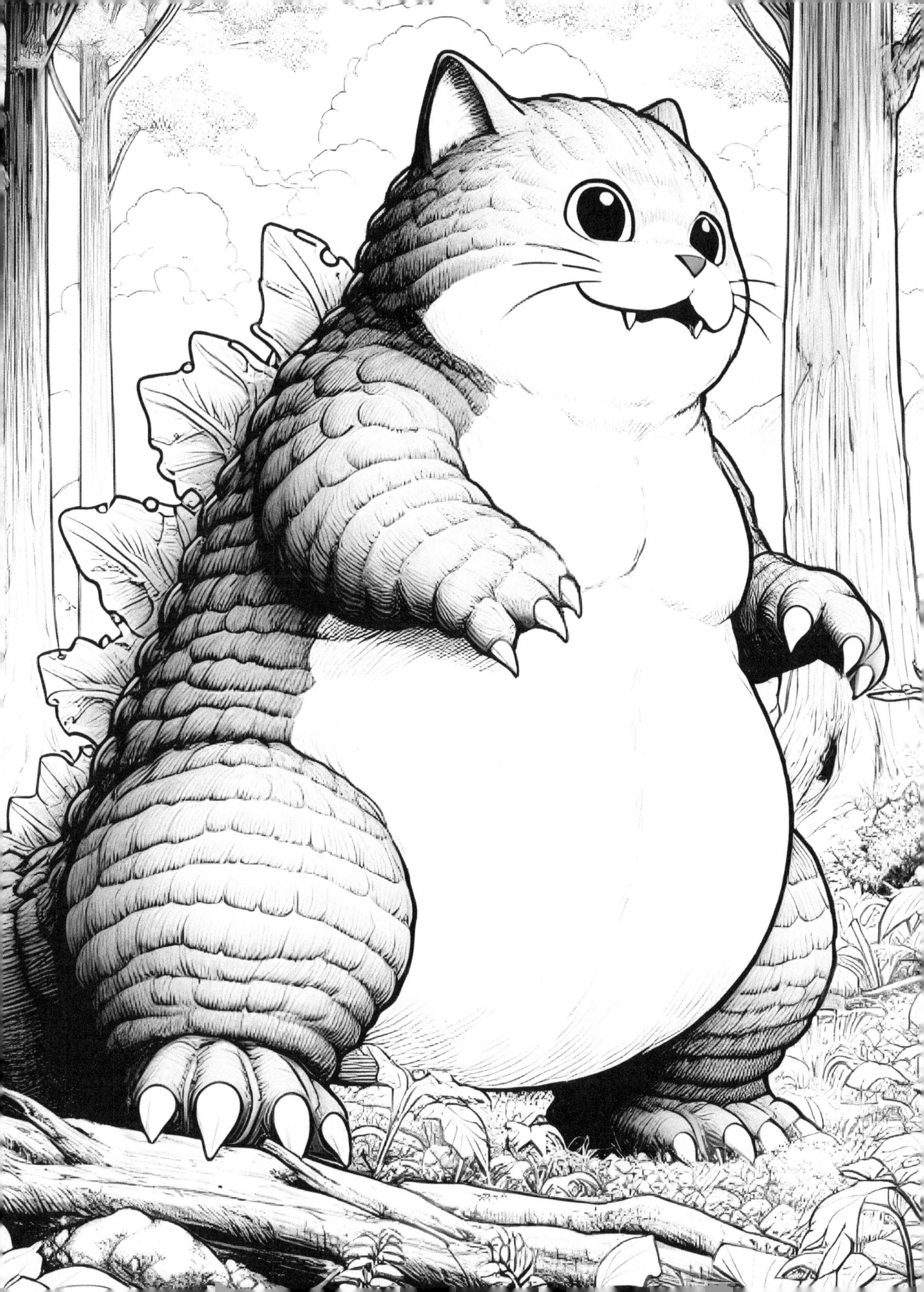

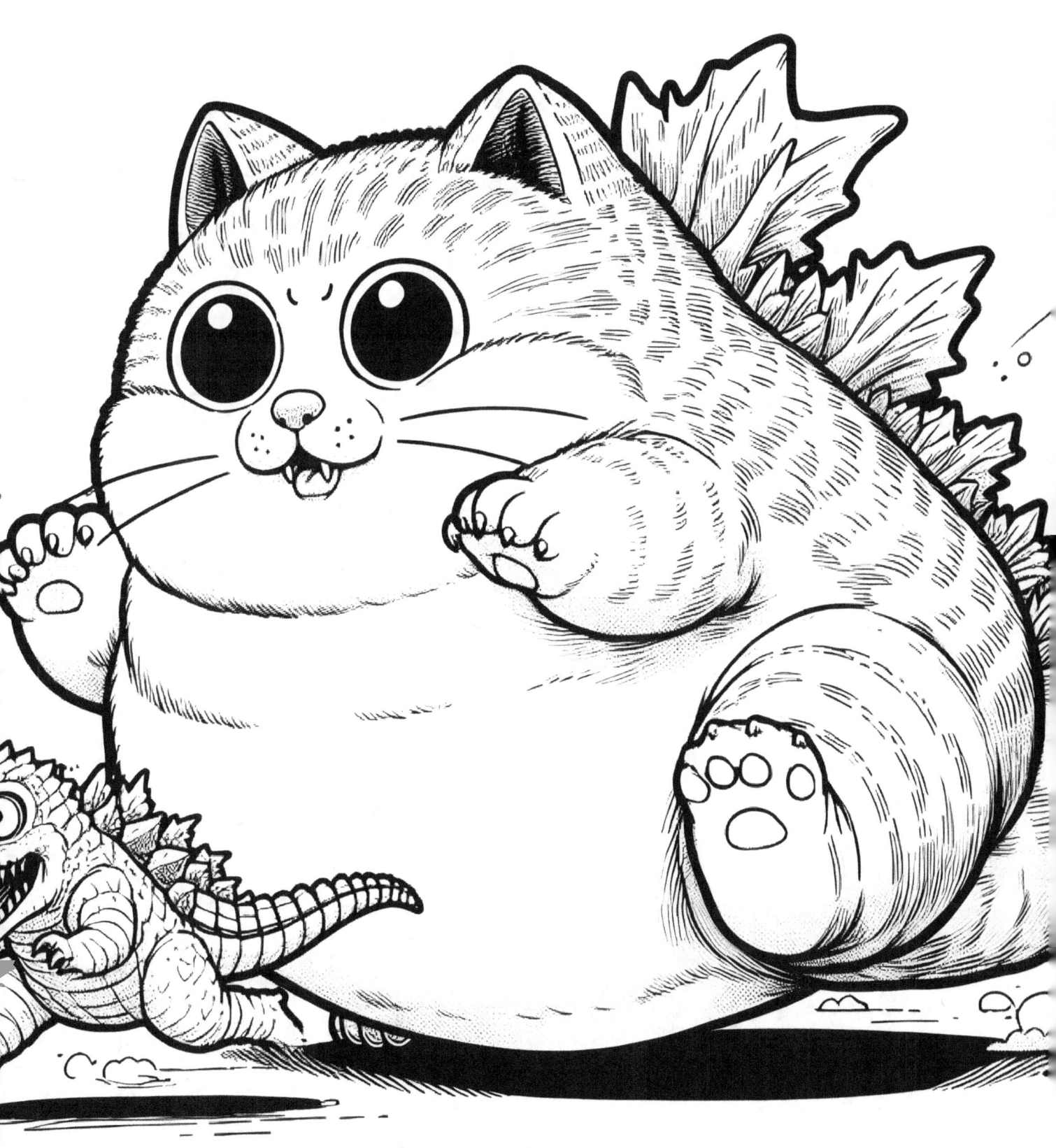

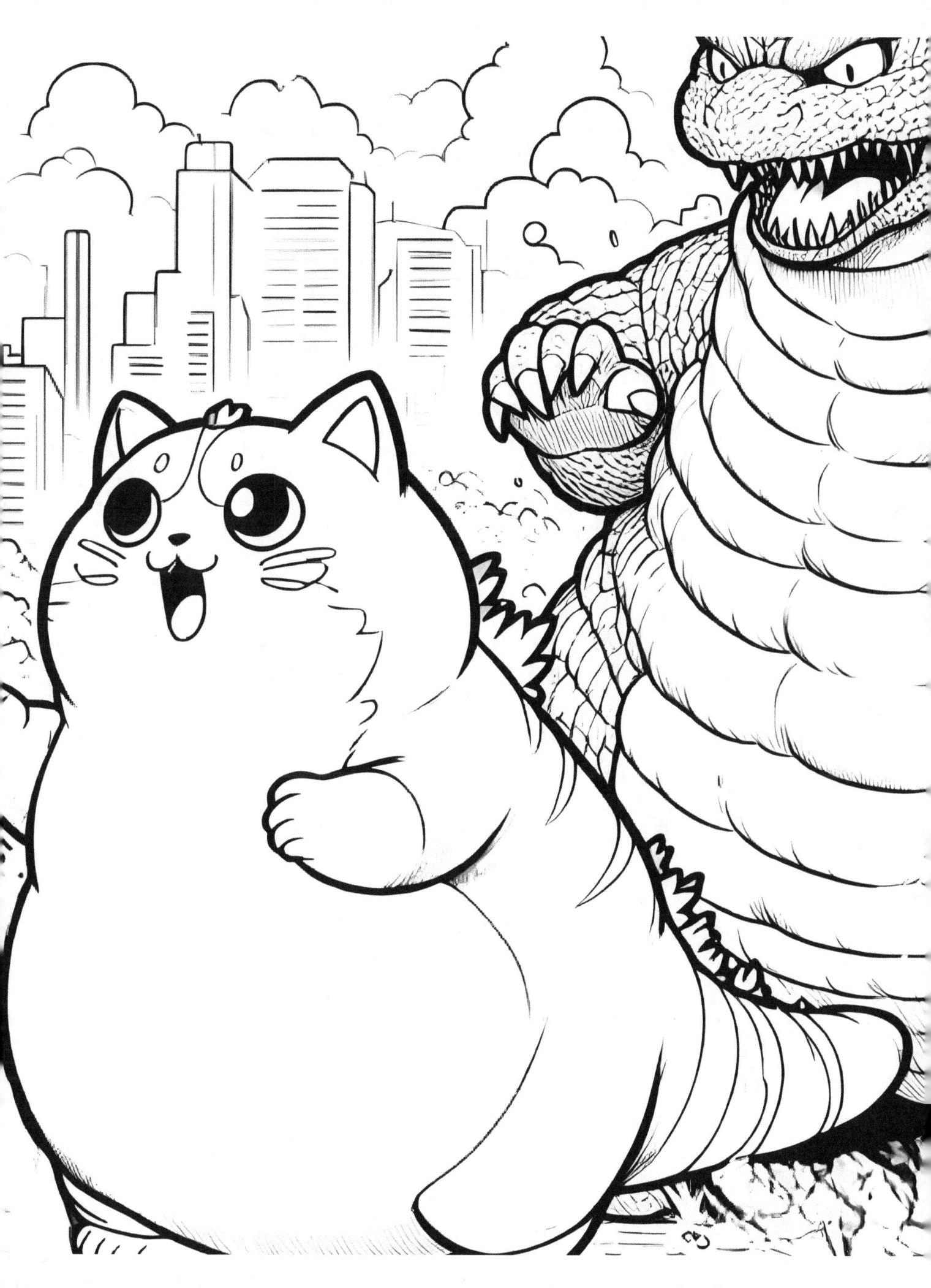

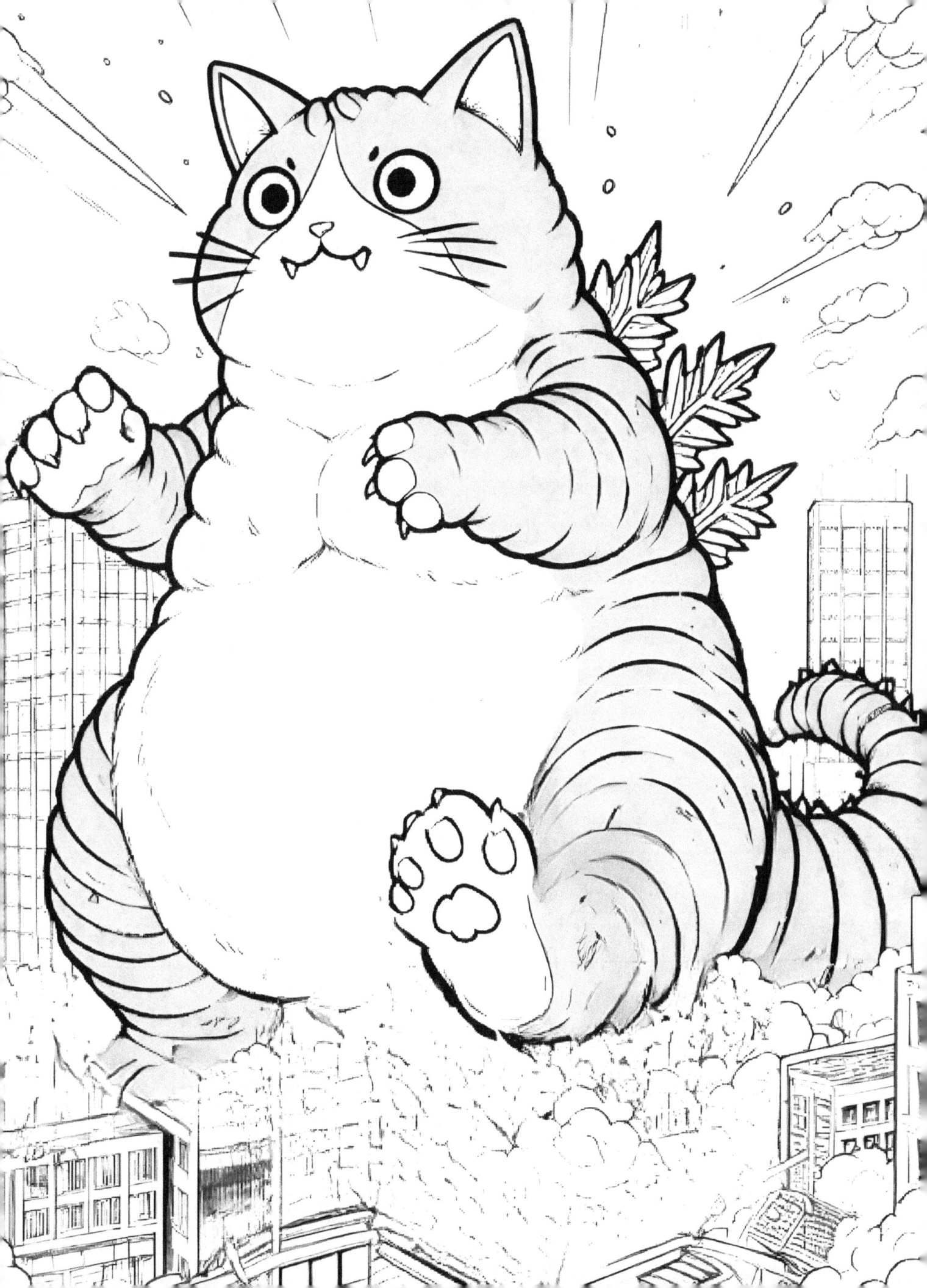

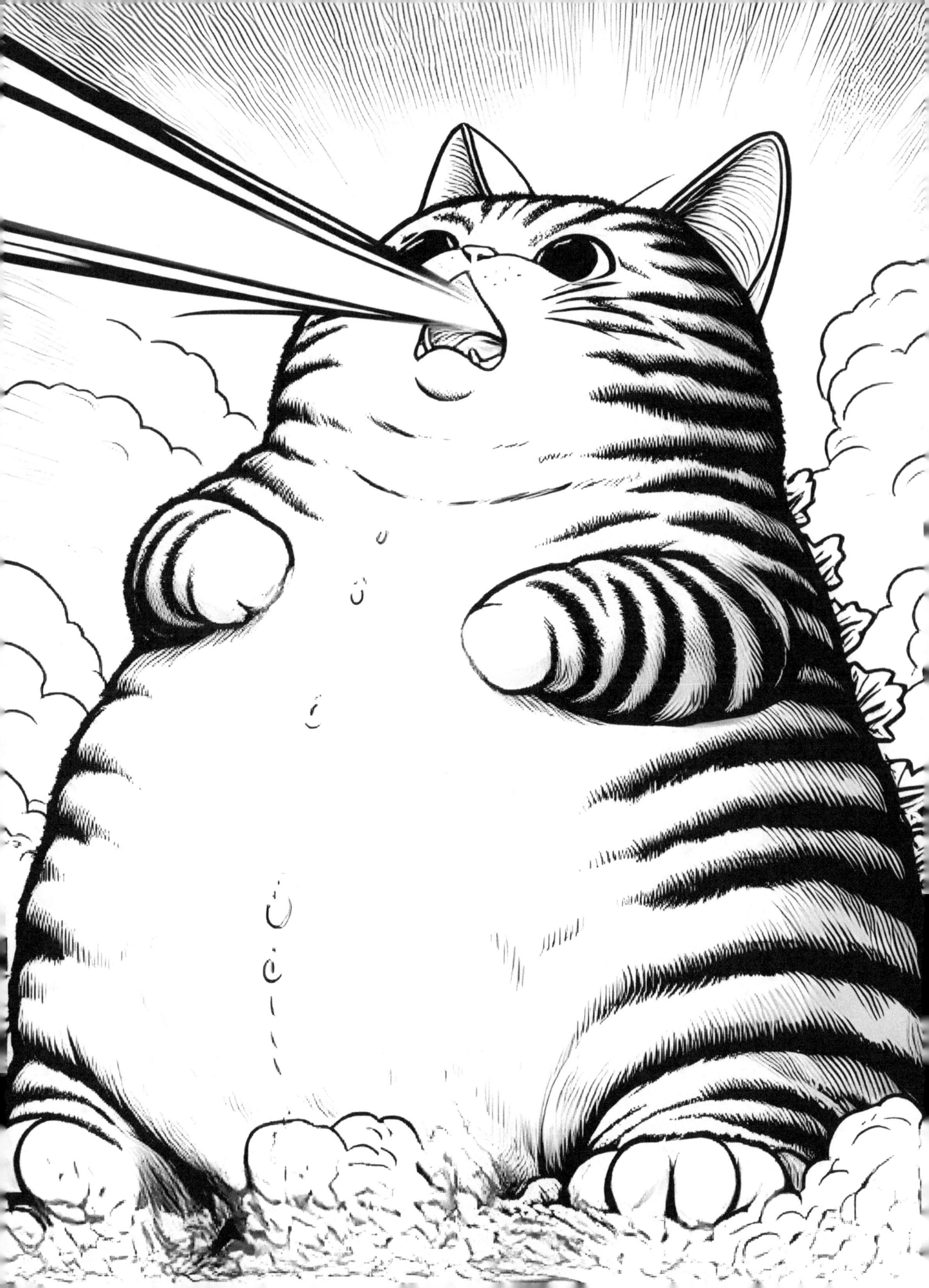

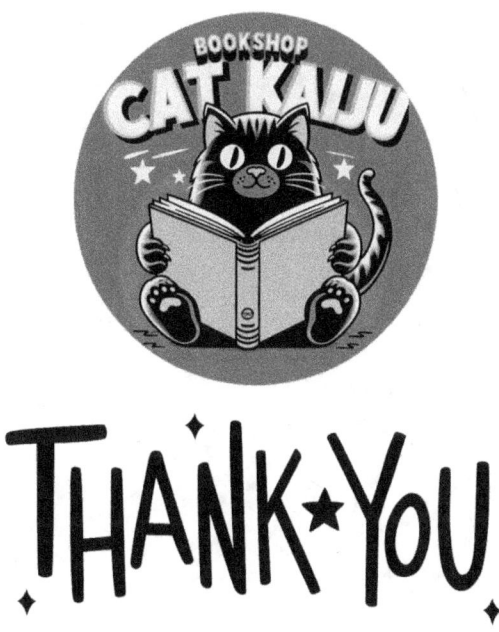

THANK★YOU

For reaching this point with our coloring book from Amazon!

We appreciate your support. If you enjoyed the experience, we'd be grateful if you could leave a review on the Amazon store page.

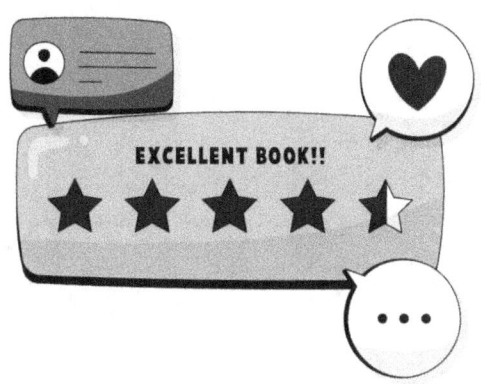

EXCELLENT BOOK!!

Exciting news! Coming soon: **CatKaiju's official merchandise store!** Get ready to rock CatKaiju gear like never before – from caps and tees to mugs and tote bags, we've got you covered!

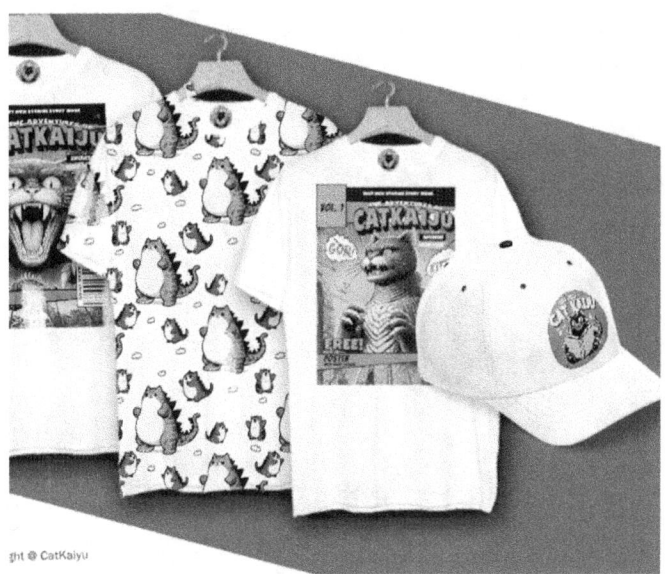

Subscribe to our newsletter for exclusive discounts and be the first to know about our grand opening date and more CatKaiju adventures. Scan the QR code or visit **https://www.catkaiju.shop/newslettersubscription** to subscribe now! Stay tuned for purrfect updates!